OMNI's
CATALOG OF THE BIZARRE

OMNI's

CATALOG OF THE BIZARRE

EDITED BY PAMELA WEINTRAUB

Photos by Olga Spiegel

An Omni Press Book
Doubleday & Company, Inc.
Garden City, New York
1985

Designed by Virginia M. Soulé

Library of Congress Cataloging in Publication Data
Main entry under title:

Omni's Catalog of the Bizarre.

"An Omni Press book."
"These articles originally appeared in Omni magazine"—
T.p. verso.
1. Curiosities and wonders—Addresses, essays,
lectures. I. Weintraub, Pamela. II. Omni (New York,
N.Y.)
AG243.W43 1985   031'.02   84-26043
ISBN 0-385-19261-4

ACKNOWLEDGEMENTS

Many people have contributed to *Omni*'s "Antimatter" column, from which this book is drawn. It is impossible to list all those who have helped us shape the sensibility of the material, lending humor, skepticism, and an appreciation of the bizarre. Below, however, is a partial list of those who have contributed to this particular volume.

Writers: Patrice Adcroft, Moira Anderson, Sherry Baker, Ben Barber, Phillip Black, Rick Boling, Robert Brody, Daniel Burstein, Jerome Clark, Margaret Coffey, Daniel Cohen, Douglas Colligan, Scott Cramer, Owen Davies, Joel Davis, Pablo F. Fenjves, Kendrick Frazier, Robert A. Freitas, Jr., Al Furst, J. Richard Greenwell, James Gorman, Sandra Hansen, Jeff Hecht, Phoebe Hoban, Patrick Huyghe, J. Allen Hynek, Kathrine Jason, Carol A. Johmann, Robert Kall, Beth Karlin, William C. Kersten, Tom Kovach, Bill Lawren, Alvin H. Lawson, Madeline Lebwohl, Irving Lieberman, Casey McCabe, Mark McCutcheon, Dave McNary, Alan Maurer, Eric Mishara, James Oberg, Henry Packer, Robert Patton, Doug Payne, James Randy, Judy Redfearn, D. Scott Rogo, Peter Rondinone, Margaret Sachs, Joel Schwartz, Robert Sheaffer, Tonia Shoumatoff, Ivor Smullen, Dava Sobel, Douglas Starr, Trent D. Stephens, Mark Teich, Carol Truxal, Marcello Truzzi, Alan Vaughan, Glenn Van Warrebey, Connie Zweig.

Special thanks must also go to Bob Guccione, Kathy Keeton, and Dick Teresi, who originally conceived of and created "Antimatter," to James Fitzgerald at Doubleday/Dolphin, who suggested the book project in the first place, and to Robert Weil, Nancy Lucas, Peter Tyson, Bev Nerenberg, Marcia Potash and Murray Cox at *Omni* for their efforts on this book. *Omni* also wishes to cite Hildegard Kron and Elizabeth Siroka for their ongoing visual contribution to the "Antimatter" column.

PREFACE

In the beginning there was matter . . . and antimatter. During the birth of our universe, many physicists believe, matter and antimatter were created in equal amounts. Yet, though antimatter can be produced in the laboratory, it is nigh unfindable in the cosmos at large.

Back in 1980 those words launched *Omni*'s first "Antimatter" column, devoted to the peculiar, the unexplainable, the mysterious, the macabre. During its first five years of existence, "Antimatter" has consistently examined the world through a trick prism, refracting science and life into rays both wondrous and bizarre. We have examined "fringe" topics from UFOs to parapsychology, from cryptozoology to the occult, maintaining a skeptical stance with the help of expert authors such as Marcello Truzzi, editor of the *Zetetic Scholar;* James Oberg, specialist on the Soviet space program; and Trent D. Stephens, biologist at Idaho State University. And if we have quoted the critics, we have also gone to their "heretical" adversaries, soliciting the opinions of researchers like J. Allen Hynek, father of the modern UFO movement, and the renowned parapsychologist, Charles Tart.

Throughout we have focused on the ironies of our subject matter, interviewing UFO cult members, feminist witches, and even transsexuals who trace their predilections to past lives. In fact, if the "Antimatter" section has had a hallmark, it is a sense of humor in the face of that strange and startling creature we call man. As we set out to do back in 1980, we have continually sought the nigh unfindable, reveling in the myriad anomalies, archetypal disturbances, and enduring mysteries that mark us all.

The "Antimatter" column forms the basis of the pages that follow. You are now entering the "Antimatter" universe, *Omni's Catalog of the Bizarre.*

—Pamela Weintraub

OMNI's

CATALOG OF THE BIZARRE

Telepathic dog: He communicates his troubles to concerned psychics.

PET TELEPATHY

Is your cat crying, your Doberman in decline? Phyllis Moline may be able to help. She's a Tennessee psychic who specializes in reading the minds of troubled animals. And, according to one Nashville shelter operator, she has already brought speedy comfort to dozens of pets, including some fifty dogs.

"We had a Great Dane," recalls Judy Myers, executive director of Action for Animals. "He was wasting away, just lying there looking at you with those big, sad eyes. Phyllis knew immediately that he was in mourning because his blanket had been taken away. When we got him a blanket, there was a total transformation. And I have a German shepherd. One of his previous owners beat him terribly, damaging his pancreas. Phyllis picked it up."

How does Moline work her miracles? "It's a matter of using the right and left brain balanced together, along with the movement of the perennial gland," she says. "A social worker gave me the scientific explanation for it, but I can never remember."

Phyllis says she's been psychic all her life but really flowered at the age of twelve, when her father was transferred to India to help build a factory. "I kept meeting gurus on the street, and they already knew my name. It was really strange." With blessings from her mother, a yogi, young Moline finally went to study in a Buddhist retreat, where she lived until her family returned to the United States five or six years later.

It doesn't take years in an ashram to learn animals' telepathy, though. "I've been giving free workshops, teaching people to communicate with animals," she reports. "They learn how to find out their pets' problems and how to make them obey when they give a command, even if they do it only in their minds."

Magic spells can bring woman-killers to justice.

FEMINIST HEX

The "trailside killer" of Marin County in California may have been caught, thanks to a hex performed by the Susan B. Anthony witch coven, at least according to Zsuzsanna Budapest, the group's high priestess.

Budapest said that the feminist coven cursed the killer, who attacked women in the wilderness, four months before the capture of suspect Joseph Carpenter. "We were looking for a place to commune with nature," Budapest explained, "and saw all these signs warning people not to walk alone at night. So, under a full moon, about thirty witches from various traditions placed a curse."

This is not the first time a witches' hex brought a woman-killer to justice, Budapest said. "Several years ago a group of us hexed a woman-killer in Gainesville, Florida. We gathered near a lake full of alligators and cursed this man, who was known for having a golden tooth that gleamed in the sun. Thirteen days later he attacked three women, who then turned on him, beat him up, and took him to the police."

Budapest would like to revive the ancient female ritual of cursing men who harm women. "I'd like to see women walk through the land with candles, placing voodoo dolls at murder sites as warnings," she said. "We have to stop killing the carriers of the race."

MAGNETIC PEOPLE?

It's common knowledge that birds, bees, and even lowly bacteria are guided by a magnetic sense. But now some scientists are claiming that people too can navigate with the help of magnetic perceptions.

The debate over whether animal magnetism is present in humans began a few years ago, when University of Manchester zoologist R. Robin Baker blindfolded some of his students, packed them into buses, and sent them on a twisting ride through the English countryside. Baker stopped the buses at various points and asked the students to indicate their starting location by pointing in a certain direction. Surprisingly they exhibited strong homing abilities.

The explanation, according to Baker, was their magnetic sixth sense. A few months later, however, several American researchers tried to reproduce Baker's results but failed.

Now Baker claims that his latest work "leaves no doubt" about the presence of a magnetic sense in human beings. Disclosing his results to *Omni,* Baker said that the American attempts were not really failures. Instead, he explains, the experiments may have been stymied by less than perfect conditions: confusing magnetic storms, the wrong time of day, and low magnetic gradients inside the buses.

To minimize these effects, Baker and his collaborator Janice Mather conducted tests in a specially constructed wooden hut. Blindfolded and earmuffed, students were seated on chairs in the middle of a dark room, turned around, and then asked to indicate their direction. After obtaining accurate answers from about 150 of his subjects, Baker is confident that he has proved his hypothesis.

Whether this latest research will convince the Americans remains to be seen. One has already called some of the data "a little bit funny."

> "It is our idleness, in
> our dreams, that the
> submerged truth sometimes
> comes to the top."
>
> —*Virginia Woolf*

TRANSSEXUAL REINCARNATION

A Van Nuys, California, group named the Alpha Gamma Project, to study possible links between reincarnation and transsexualism, was awarded a three-year, $450,000 grant, by a private foundation.

Psychologist Nancy Ledins, a transsexual and former Roman Catholic priest who directs this project, is studying 450 transsexual men and women to "try to determine whether reincarnational imprinting tends to short-circuit current life-styles for some people."

After a personal experience that suggested such a link might exist, Ledins said, "I decided that if I ever got a chance to pursue it, I would. I got the opportunity through this grant."

Now in its first year, the study is hampered by negative publicity, Ledins said. "Every time something appears, I spend three months shoring up the dike before I can get back to research. Some people don't like what we're doing."

Yet Ledins does believe the study might help explain why certain people have trouble adjusting to their gender and why they undergo sex-change operations.

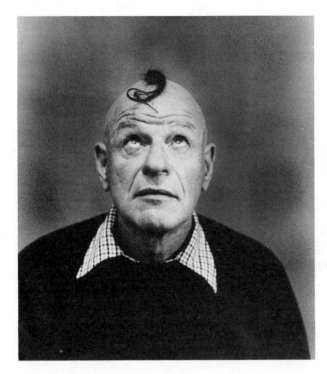

Can this man grow a new head of hair with the help of laser beams?

LASER VS. BALDNESS?

If the purveyors of balding "cures" come across some recent Chinese research, the next useless thing applied to bald spots may be the laser beam.

According to the Chinese-language *Laser Journal,* scientists from Guangdong Province shaved hair from two areas on each of twelve guinea pigs. They illuminated one area on each animal with an infrared laser for a minute a day and left the other shaved area alone. After twenty days the researchers found that hair grew faster in the laser-treated areas: 0.71 millimeter per day on the average versus 0.59 millimeter per day in the untreated areas. In addition there were more hair follicles and hair was "thicker, longer, and more uniform" in the laser-treated spots.

What works on guinea pigs with normal hair, however, won't necessarily work on men whose hair has stopped growing. The Chinese study did *not* mention human baldness. But a lack of scientific evidence probably won't prevent charlatans from marketing the "laser" cure.

Karma Construction began Nixon's bathroom with a purification ritual.

NIXON'S
BATHROOM

If you can get good karma from a kitchen and a bathroom, Richard Nixon ought to have plenty when he's in his New York office.

A company called Karma Construction submitted the low bid of $9,300 and was hired by the General Services Administration to build a private kitchen and bathroom for Nixon's new office.

The firm's motto is "We build mantra-filled walls." The company's founder, thirty-nine-year-old Barry Bryant, employs about twenty workers, craftsmen, artists, and spiritual seekers who "believe in meditation in action."

Using the Tibetan Buddhist mandala—which assigns a color to each aspect of human personality—as a guide, Bryant chose blue for the bathroom and yellow for the kitchen. "Blue represents anger and yellow, pride," Bryant notes. "By contemplating these colors, one transforms anger and pride into equanimity."

Work on the project began with a purification ritual, which included burning incense, chanting mantras, and performing symbolic finger gestures. Ancient texts and Chinese and Tibetan relics were sealed in plastic bags behind the sheetrock walls, which also conceal written mantras.

"We felt the impact of building something for a former president," Bryant says. "The colors, tiles, and textures look as if they belong in a château. We really felt we were building a monument."

This jail cell, with walls painted institution-gray, will ruin the morale of inhabitants.

"Round about what is, lies a whole mysterious world of might be, a psychological romance of possibilities and things that do not happen."

—*Henry Wadsworth Longfellow*

PINK JAILS

Jails and prisons are violent places, but a new technique in penology may alleviate the tension. The idea is simple: Just paint all the cells pink.

The Sweetwater, Florida, Police Department has already painted its jail pink and claims the color has a calming effect on hostile prisoners. "It really works," said Lieutenant Bud Dawson, who got the idea from a news report about an experiment in California in which mental patients and hostile prisoners were calmed by pink rooms.

Sergeant Ray Toledo has seen more than twenty prisoners locked up in the cell since its color change. "Several prisoners came into the jail in a rage, and after a couple of minutes in the cell they calmed down. One hostile prisoner came into the cell and cried for two hours," he claimed.

Mouse/chicken hybrid.

CHICKEN TEETH

In an experiment being cited as evidence that evolution may sometimes proceed by rapid species-changing leaps, a University of Connecticut biologist has managed, through a series of macrogenetic experiments conducted over a number of years, to grow chicken teeth—in mice.

Edward Kollar said that British embryologist Dame Honour Fell discovered that teeth begin to form in five-day-old chick embryos but disappear by the sixth day.

So Kollar joined embryonic chick cells with molar connective tissue from nude mice, a strain of mice that have no thymus gland and therefore do not reject foreign tissue. The mouse cells activated the dormant chick-teeth gene. Several weeks later reptilelike teeth appeared in the mice, complete with enamel layers.

"The experiment is being interpreted by a new group of evolutionary biologists as evidence that a new species formation may be a macro- rather than a microgenetic event," Kollar says. "They claim major changes occur because of sudden, severe, probably developmental phenomena that can produce new forms."

Kollar has studied tooth development for fifteen years, but he has always felt hampered by the lack of "a good dental mutant." Very often, he explains, insights into normal processes can be derived from mutant aberrations. Unfortunately mutant teeth rarely develop. "When they do occur," says Kollar, "they are so devastating to the animal that it doesn't survive." Now, thanks to his experiment, biologists may have an evolutionary dental mutant to study.

Next Kollar is considering an attempt to join mouse cells with live chick embryos to see whether the chicks will be able to grow their own teeth.

> "It is a sign of the ambivalence people feel toward science that scientists are often villains in science fiction."
>
> —*Isaac Asimov*

PIZZA GHOST

Most hauntings seem to take place in ancient castles, Victorian garrets, and other old buildings with strange and perhaps violent pasts. But recently in Santa Ana, California, a ghost reportedly wreaked havoc inside a pizza-manufacturing plant.

Several employees of Sabatasso Foods claimed to have seen the ethereal figure, and all gave the same description—the ghost was a dark-complexioned man, about 5'9" tall, with a moustache, a white smock, and a hard hat.

"When I was first told that a security guard had seen this ghost, my reaction was 'What's this guy been smoking?' " recalls Louis Sabatasso, president of the company. "Then the lights began coming on at night by themselves. And we have a $50,000 utility bill each month under normal circumstances. So I knew something had to be done."

Sabatasso acted by securing the services of psychic Nonie Fagatt, who conducts tours of haunted castles in England for British Caledonian Airways and was a consultant for the movie *Ghostbusters.*

"In the film there's a ghost in a refrigerator and the ghost in the pizza plant retreated into the freezer. So I was afraid people might think this was some kind of publicity gimmick," she asserts. "But it was very serious."

Fagatt planned her exorcism for the very next week, but before she could act even stranger things began to happen. A burglar alarm was sounded and the company's security system couldn't turn it off. When the plant was opened on Monday, workers found that the huge pallets loaded with frozen pizzas had been scattered around the room. An electric crane was moving back and forth by itself, without any sign of an operator. And one of the giant pizza freezer doors was inexplicably banging against another door.

To force the spirit to leave, Fagatt took one of the witnesses and Sabatasso Foods public relations representative Sherrie Kerr into the room-sized freezer. The three prayed, spread salt to attract "ectoplasmic vapors," and lit a candle. Fagatt contacted the apparition mentally, she says, and learned that he was the ghost of a man who worked in the factory when it was a meat-processing plant.

After being killed in an accident elsewhere, he had returned to his former place of employment, only to find a pizza plant in its stead.

After a massive effort on her part, Fagatt claims, the spirit left. "I felt a rush of energy," she explains. "My neck was injured, as though I received a karate chop at the back of my head."

Though this particular ghost is gone, however, the hauntings are not completely over. In fact several Sabatasso workers have spotted a shadowy figure lurking on top of the building. "There's another ghost up on the roof," Fagatt asserts. "But I don't want to crawl up there after it."

"The ghost that got into our
house on the night of
November 17, 1915, raised
such a hullabaloo of
misunderstandings that I
am sorry I didn't just let it
keep on walking, and go
to bed."

—*James Thurber*

There may be a ghost atop the Sabatasso
Food Factory in Santa Ana, California.

A cigar-shaped object was seen over the mountains of Reserve, New Mexico.

> "Luscomb saw a
> mammoth cigar-shaped object as
> long as four 747s
> glide easily across the sky."

UFO
UPDATE

The sun set over the mountains of Reserve, New Mexico, and soon the stars were shining bright. Then suddenly the early evening calm was shattered by the sound of four jets swooping through the mountain passes. The pilots were clearly searching for something. And Dan Luscomb thought he knew what it was.

Just an hour earlier, on that evening of December 8, 1981, Luscomb had allegedly witnessed a cigar-shaped object glide effortlessly across the twilight sky. It was "as big as four 747s linked together," recalls Luscomb, who owns the Whispering Pines Resort seven miles south of Reserve. "A jet was in pursuit, straining to keep up with the thing," Luscomb adds. "But every time the plane got close, the object slipped away."

Luscomb's account was soon picked up by a reporter from the nearby El Paso *Times*. The tiny article might have gone virtually unnoticed, but as it turned out, J. Allen Hynek, director of the Center for UFO Studies, in Evanston, Illinois, chose just that day to visit his private New Mexico observatory. He was driving through the city of El Paso when he picked up a copy of the *Times* and read the story.

A few months later Hynek decided to investigate by visiting Reserve itself. In the days that followed, he interviewed dozens of local people. Nine witnesses in all, he found, swore they'd seen the cigar-shaped object just about the same time as Luscomb did.

Lance Swapp, for instance, declared he saw a bright light while driving home from his job at Jake's Grocery Store in the neighboring town of Luna. "When I got home," Swapp recalls, "my brother was hollering at me to look up in the sky. There was a large object over our heads, with a jet on its trail." And housewife Alma Hobbs, who was on her way to Luscomb's resort, said she observed a red ball rising from the ground. Within seconds it apparently turned sideways to resemble a tube.

The Federal Aviation Administration, Hynek soon discovered, claimed that it had picked up nothing unusual on its radar screen that night, and the

Air Force said it had dispatched no jets to the area. Nevertheless Hynek was convinced that the people of Reserve and Luna were on the level, and he set out to see whether he could determine what the unidentified object was.

Back at his center in Chicago, however, he found himself rejecting one theory after another. Because of the object's shape, for example, some people suggested it was a missile. But missiles make a deafening noise, and this object was silent. Others said the mysterious object might be a military test vehicle. But Hynek contends that "no known technology can make a ninety-degree turn in seconds, as this object allegedly did. The feat," he adds, "defies Newton's Second Law of Motion."

Whatever the object is, Hynek concludes, it doesn't seem like something constructed by man. As for the Air Force officials' denial, he believes "it would embarrass them to admit there was something in the skies they did not understand."

"To know is nothing at all; to imagine is everything."

—*Anatole France*

FLYING
CARPETS

As part of his otherwise serious research into superconducting materials, a California college professor at Stanford University, physicist William A. Little, has suggested a whimsical use for superconductors: the flying carpet.

Speaking at the Quantum Theory Conference at the University of Florida, he proposed that all kinds of fantastic things would be possible with a superconducting material that operates at room temperature (present superconductors work only at very low temperatures).

Using a sort of magnetic levitation, you could float cars over superconductor highways, transmit electricity thousands of miles with no loss, and, if you had a mind to, weave flying carpets from the material.

First you would weave a large wall-to-wall carpet in a magnetic field, to trap some of the field in the carpet. You'd lay that down on the floor of the room and then weave a series of smaller rugs in another magnetic field. If these small rugs were laid over the larger one, they would float.

Each one, Little estimates, would hover about a yard above the floor and could float around easily, carrying a 200-pound man.

It might even be possible to use the same method to weave superconductor clothes. "Then you could fly around the room."

Little often uses the flying carpet example in his talks and lectures, and this usually interests everyone. But there are some exceptions. "When word of this first came out," he recalls, "I got letters from practitioners of Transcendental Meditation who wrote something like, 'What's the big deal? We've been doing this for years.' "

Leatherlike box: It carries messages to God.

GODBOX

There is now a direct mail service to God. According to Marge Haley of Little Rock, Arkansas, and Geri Nielson and Jerry Goossen of San Diego, all you have to do is write out your request on a preprinted form and place it in a white, "leatherlike" container stamped with the legend "GODBOX."

Haley, Nielson, and Goossen market the box for $14.95 through A Creative Company, based in Carson City, Nevada. All profits, Goossen emphasizes, are earmarked for an unnamed children's charity.

Geri Nielson came up with the original idea for the Godbox back in 1982 when, following a series of personal tragedies, she decided to stuff her prayer requests into an envelope. Her two friends soon tried the method as well, and all three claim their prayers were answered.

Haley speculates that the box works because "it gives you a sense of perspective. You can see your problems in black and white, and it gives you a sense of relief. If you decide you can solve a problem better than God, you simply remove that request."

Goossen has a more metaphysical explanation: "I think there are a bunch of unseen beings around us all the time," she says. "They are angels and they rejuvenate our bodies while we sleep. They will do our bidding, but first we need to get our problems out of our heads and write down what we want them to do."

What do religious leaders think of this new technique?

"In Buddhism they put prayers on a prayer wheel, and Catholics place intentions on altars," notes James Hopewell, an expert on comparative religion who teaches at Emory University's Candler School of Theology. "Out of context such things may seem pretty silly. But they can be very meaningful for the people doing them."

M. G. McLuhan, associate pastor of the Mount Paran Church of God in Atlanta, takes a harsher view. "The Godbox," he says, "is a striking example of spiritually irresponsible gimmickry."

But Goossen, who claims his critics are "self-serving," disagrees. "The Godbox could put organized religion out of business," he says. "With the Godbox, you just go to God and ask for what you want. And you get it."

"In my view, ESP's return to
respectability has so
widened the scope of
imagination and brought
back areas of wonder and
mystery long lost to the
disenchanting forces of
science and materialism."

—*Martyn Skinner*

17

Electrodes may help researchers fine-tune the art of hypnotic regression therapy.

EMOTIONAL ALARM CLOCK

Hypnotic regression, the therapy of experiencing earlier life traumas to obtain insights into psychological problems, has always had one complication. The therapist has not always known the best point to stop the regression. Now New York psychologist Ivan Wentworth-Rohr has come up with something that can do just that. He calls it an emotional alarm clock.

Wentworth-Rohr, chief of the behavioral therapy unit at St. Vincent's Hospital in New York City, uses electrodes to monitor the most responsive body systems, watching for changes in muscles or sweat glands, as a patient is regressed. When Wentworth-Rohr's machine senses a surge of activity in the monitored area, it sets off an alarm.

In one session, for example, Wentworth-Rohr had a patient imagine he was walking through his childhood home. The alarm went off when he reached the foot of the hall stairs. "This showed it was an emotionally loaded area," the psychologist declares. "Then I had the patient regress in time to an earlier age. The alarm went off at two years old, a point at which the patient had had a traumatic experience. The patient remembered being left untended, feeling isolated and alone."

Wentworth-Rohr thinks his alarm might be valuable for other forms of psychotherapy as well. "There's a good possibility that your body remembers more straightforwardly than your mind."

BOG MURDER

Police in the British town of Chester had long suspected that Peter Reyn-Bardt, fifty-seven, could explain the disappearance of his wife, Malika, who was last seen twenty-two years ago. But authorities had no evidence until last spring, when workers digging in a peat bog near Reyn-Bardt's home made a grizzly discovery—they found a woman's skull with hair and an eyeball still attached, the yellowing remains of a brain visible inside the head.

Convinced they had Malika's remains, Chester detectives confronted Peter Reyn-Bardt, who promptly confessed to the murder. Malika, he claimed, drove him to the crime by threatening to expose his homosexuality.

The admitted murderer was arrested and jailed. But one month before his trial, the case took a strange turn. Analyzing the skull, experts from Oxford University learned it had belonged to a woman who died around 410 A.D., when the Romans were still in the region.

Despite the fact that his wife's real body was never unearthed, Peter Reyn-Bardt was recently found guilty of killing Malika and sentenced to life imprisonment.

"The skull had been preserved in the peat bog for around sixteen centuries and obviously has nothing to do with Malika Reyn-Bardt," prosecutor Martin Thomas told the court. "But its discovery led directly to the arrest of the defendant. It was the supreme irony."

The probability of thinking about a person five minutes before reading his obituary may be as high as 3 parts in 100,000.

COINCIDENCE

Improbable-sounding coincidences are often put forth as evidence of thought transference, or telepathy. The Nobel laureate physicist Luis W. Alvarez once was startled by a coincidence that happened to him.

Reading a newspaper one day, he came across a phrase that triggered associations and led to his thinking of a person from his college days, "very probably for the first time in thirty years." Five minutes later in the same newspaper, he came across an obituary notice reporting the death of that person. Many people would have jumped to the conclusion that clairvoyance or precognition had been responsible.

Not Alvarez. He realized that the coincidence was a coincidence and, like the good scientist that he is, he proceeded to calculate the chances of its happening. He found that the probability of thinking about a person five minutes before learning of that person's death is about 3 parts in 100,000 per year. Multiplying by the 100 million adults in the United States, an incredible 3,000 such experiences of the sort should occur every year, or about 10 per day.

In a letter to *Science* entitled "A Pseudo Experience in Parapsychology," Alvarez concluded: "With such a large sample to draw from, it is not surprising that some exceedingly astonishing coincidences are reported in the parapsychological literature as proof of extrasensory perception in one form or another."

Psychics who burn candles
may be ripping you off.

"The usual question is,
'What is the use of so many planets
as we see about the sun?'
To which the answer is, that they
are worlds or places of habitation."

—*William Derham*

PSYCHIC
BETTER BUSINESS
BUREAU

The Association of Psychic Practitioners, in San Jose, California, wants to become the Better Business Bureau of the psychic profession.

According to Mary Palermo, president of the association, many so-called psychics and fortune-tellers lack integrity. "They may make a client think they can change his life," she says. "We have no evidence that that is possible.

"There are some in this area, for instance, who claim that by burning candles, they can bring a lover to you. And the candles come high, as much as five hundred dollars. I don't like being bunched with the kind of people who burn candles."

The association is working with psychologists, business consultants, and "reputable" psychics in an attempt to establish criteria for certifying psychics who practice their art in an ethical manner."

MERMEN
AND MERMAIDS

When Waldemar Lehn saw an armless figure with a bulging head rise above the surface of Lake Winnipeg in Canada, he knew exactly what he was looking at. It was a merman, and he took a photo to prove it.

Lehn's picture, in combination with a clever computer program, showed that ancient sailors who reported mermaids and mermen were telling the truth. The men did see something: ordinary marine creatures whose images were distorted by changes in the atmosphere.

Lehn, an electrical engineer at the University of Manitoba, developed a computer program to simulate image distortions under a variety of weather conditions. When he duplicated stormy-weather images of a walrus and a killer whale on the computer, he wound up with merman shapes. Thus he concluded that sea mammals, seen in a storm, would fit the descriptions of half-human and half-fish creatures.

The cause of the distortion, according to Lehn, is a temperature inversion that occurs when a mass of warm air moves over cold air. This bends the light so that objects are distorted beyond the horizon. As the inversion disintegrates, the image begins to look fuzzy.

As for the merman of Lake Winnipeg, Lehn finally learned that it was a foot-high boulder on the shore of the lake.

Modern-day chimpanzee: Were his ancestors protohuman?

ASCENT OF MAN

Jeremy Cherfas and John Gribbin, two British science writers, are monkeying around with a new theory of evolution. The monkey descended from man, they suggest, not vice versa.

Their argument is based on evidence that the DNA in both monkeys and humans was rather alike a mere 4.5 million years ago. This contradicts the fossil record, which suggests that a close kinship between man and monkey has not existed for 20 million years.

To account for the new genetic evidence, Cherfas and Gribbin hypothesized that approximately 4.5 million years ago a common ancestor of man, chimpanzee, and gorilla—a race of walking apes—split into two groups. One branch adapted itself to a rigorous life on the plains, eventually evolving into upright protohumans. The other branch preferred to hang out in the trees and eat fruit. They "de-evolved" into the simians of today.

If this sounds like sheer monkey business, it is. "We don't really believe in the descending-ape theory," Cherfas says. "We simply wanted to show how many gray areas there are in fossil evidence. We'd like paleontologists to consult the molecular clock and then reconsider their findings."

So far the writers have heard from preachers and politicians, but the fossil people have remained silent.

23

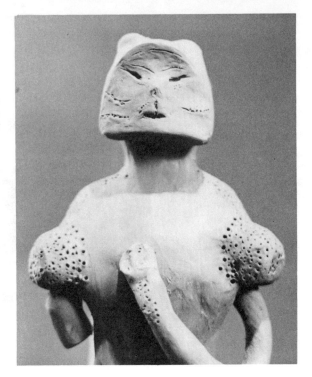

Mysterious artifact:
Fertility god or message
from space?

DOGU
SPACE SUITS

Dogus are small clay statues with pointy heads, insect eyes, and torsos marked by intricate patterns of dots and stripes. They were made in Japan between 7000 and 520 B.C. Some people think they represent Japanese fertility gods. But, according to Vaughn Greene, author of the book *Astronauts of Ancient Japan,* these artifacts actually depict spacesuit-clad visitors from another planet. The most striking evidence to date, Greene says, is the similarity between dogu markings and the new NASA spacesuit—the extravehicular mobility unit (EMU)—to be worn by space shuttle astronauts outside their ship.

For instance, Greene says, the chest-pack control units on the EMU are in roughly the same place as circular knobs on a dogu chest. These knobs probably controlled life-support systems on the dogu spacesuit, he asserts, just as they do on the EMU. And the stripes surrounding the dogu knobs are simply markers to calibrate the quantity of water or oxygen being dispensed to the person in the spacesuit. Greene theorizes that the top and bottom of the dogu spacesuit were put on separately, just as the EMU is.

One NASA scientist notes that an advanced civilization would probably design spacesuits far more sophisticated than what Greene sees on the dogu. But Greene suggests that if our spacesuits could get us to the moon, they could also get us to another planet.

> "A pair of robots
> hooked onto his trouser legs
> and dragged him
> in the direction of the dome."

UFO UPDATE

Curiosity seekers still find their way to Bob Taylor's doorstep, fifteen miles west of Edinburgh, Scotland. They come to hear of the morning of November 9, 1979, when the usually phlegmatic forester, pants torn and voice gasping, stumbled from the rolling woodland near his home. He'd been attacked by two robots from a spacecraft, he told his incredulous wife, who retorted, "There's not such a thing!"

Those words stung the sixty-one-year-old Scotsman, and he felt compelled to prove his credibility. So he picked up the phone and called Sergeant Ian Wark, a policeman in the town of Livingston.

At ten that morning, Taylor told Wark, he had been inspecting livestock fencing. He'd just walked down a timberland path and turned into a clearing when he saw a "domed spacecraft as tall as the surrounding spruces." As he stood transfixed, Taylor claims, a pair of small, "robotlike balls" rolled toward him, each one bristling with half a dozen metallic spikes, or legs, that made "plopping noises" as they touched the ground. Next the robots hooked onto his trouser legs and dragged him in the direction of the dome. "Suddenly a powerful smell choked me," Taylor recalls. "Then I lost consciousness." He awoke in the clearing a short time later, alone, with a blinding headache and unsteady legs.

Returning to the spot that afternoon with Wark, Taylor pointed to a pair of ten-foot-long bulldozer tracks set seven feet apart. Encircling the tracks were thirty-two holes, each three inches in diameter and three inches deep. Taylor saw the imprints as the unmistakable mark of a spacecraft. But to Sergeant Wark, they were an enigma, one that deserved serious investigation.

The sergeant spent days trying to locate earthly machinery that would leave tracks of identical dimensions. When he failed to find any, he sent the forester's clothes to a forensic laboratory, again without results.

Wark contends that Taylor's story cannot be dismissed, but he isn't the sole sleuth on the case. The day after the incident architect Steuart Campbell, an investigator for the British UFO Research Association, arrived on the

Spiked balls: Are these the aliens that attacked an Edinburgh man?

scene. In his recent report Campbell concludes that Taylor witnessed ball lightning, a rare electrical discharge that now and again flashes across the sky.

But a lot of people have been calling Campbell's theory rubbish. Among his detractors is Bob Taylor, who reasons, "If it was some kind of lightning, there would have been severe heat and burned grass." J. Dale Barry, a laser physicist and ball-lightning expert at Hughes Aircraft Company, agrees. The maximum diameter reported for ball lightning is thirty centimeters, Barry notes, while the circle formed in Livingston was many times that size.

Bob Taylor's story is still repeated by Livingston schoolchildren, who know him as "the man that saw the UFO." Now retired, he often returns to the familiar forest clearing. "The spot seems to be a magnet, and I'm drawn there," he says. "I can't imagine this happening twice, but if it did, that would be lovely."

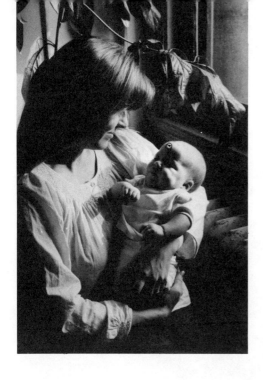

Can a newborn baby take note of its mother's hairstyle and emotional state?

REMEMBERING BIRTH

In our mother's womb we were kept warm and secure. No pain, no fear, just peace and quiet, and a comforting heartbeat to soothe us. Then, suddenly, we were thrust into a new environment. Noise, light, pain, terror—all came crashing down on us at once. To say the least, being born was traumatic. Why then don't we remember that event?

"The fact is," says clinical psychologist David Chamberlain, "we do." Chamberlain, of the Anxiety Treatment Center in San Diego, hypnotized children and found they remembered their birth in detail. Many recalled their mother's hairstyle and emotional state, the surgical instruments used, and even conversations among hospital attendants.

In most cases, according to Chamberlain, descriptions given by both mother and child were nearly identical. "The accuracy of recall," he says, "suggests sophisticated mental activity from the beginning of life."

Most other obstetricians and psychologists say, "Hogwash!" They attribute these "memories" to pure fantasy, explaining that infants simply do not have the intellectual ability to remember anything occurring so early. Nevertheless Chamberlain is adamant. His research has convinced him, he says, that "memory probably can go all the way back to the womb and may even go back as far as conception."

Psychic burnout can be
eased with vitamins A, B₂,
and zinc.

NUTRITION FOR PSYCHICS

Sensitive to the psychic energies of the universe? If so, you probably suffer from a debilitating condition known as psychic burnout. Fortunately there is a cure. According to Bill Wachsmuth, chief pharmacist for the Payless Drugstore in Mountain View, California, all you need is a prescription for vitamins.

Addressing a local occult group on the special nutritional needs of psychics, Wachsmuth explained that persons "open" to the energies surrounding them are particularly prone to stress. He reasons that they utilize B-complex and C vitamins far more rapidly than those who are "closed" to the energies.

The nutritional needs of each psychic depend upon the kind of "hocus-pocus" he or she does, Wachsmuth said. For example, a clairvoyant, who "sees" things at a distance, will deplete the nutrients needed by the eye, vitamins A and B_2 and zinc. A medium who "talks" to spirits may suffer from sore throats and a corresponding deficiency of iodine.

Wachsmuth added that clairaudiants—people who "hear" distant sounds —suffer from a different problem: an excess of earwax. They can revitalize their powers simply by cleaning their ears.

Clown from Kansas: He has a black van and a sinister grin.

KILLER CLOWNS

If a masked man in a clown suit tries to lure you into his van, don't go, says Loren Coleman, a Boston writer who specializes in unexplained phenomena.

According to Coleman, reports of "sinister-looking adults dressed like clowns have been surfacing in the national press for quite a while." Most of the clowns, seen in cities from Newark, New Jersey, to Omaha, drive black vans, Coleman says.

Coleman, who says his information comes from newspaper clippings and interviews with people, doesn't have any explanation for the phenomenon. "These clowns could be real people or hallucinations in the minds of children," he suggests. "They could even be three-dimensional images created by the collective unconscious of the masses."

Reporters at the Kansas City *Star*, who called the costumed men "killer clowns" in a recent article, are also puzzled. "The cops said it was a lot of baloney, just a bunch of kids with wild imaginations," says one *Star* staffer. "Still, we had all these terrified parents phoning us at the newspaper."

Police in Pittsburgh are more sanguine. "We had calls about bunny rabbits, clowns, and even a Spiderman," one detective on night duty recalls. "But these characters were never seen by police. The calls themselves could have been hoaxes."

"We had one clown who exposed himself," adds a detective in Brockton, Massachusetts. "He was never apprehended, but it ruined the whole image of the circus for our kids."

MODERN-DAY
VOODOO

Want revenge? Then punish your enemy with a voodoo hex. According to psychiatrist Ken Golden of the University of Arkansas Medical School in Little Rock, people who *believe* they are under a spell sometimes manifest real medical afflictions.

In recent years Golden has identified two dozen hospital patients whose ailments, including cardiac arrest, hysterical paralysis, and uncontrollable muscle spasms, were psychosomatically caused by black magic spells. "I am convinced," he says, "that these cases represent a minuscule fraction of what is going on."

Golden became fascinated with voodoo after meeting medicine men during his Peace Corps stint in Ghana. When he arrived at the University of Arkansas, he realized that many rural blacks, like the Africans, had some of their health needs answered by local voodoo practitioners.

Since then he has become a "voodoo consultant." When hexed patients don't respond to prescribed medical remedies, Golden treats them with hypnosis, psychotherapy, or placebos—brilliantly colored liquids that the ailing believe are omnipotent.

Some Chinese children claim they can read with their armpits.

CHINA'S ARMPIT SAVANTS

Wang Qiang, twelve, and Wang Bin, ten, use ESP to "read" the messages tucked under their armpits, according to a report in *Nature Journal,* China's prestigious science magazine. Indeed the publication even arranged a conference so that the sisters could demonstrate their powers. Performing before a scientific audience, they seemed to describe the scribbled messages stuffed in their armpits, in their hands, and even in their ears.

The seminar piqued the interest of Luo Dongsu, a Chinese Air Force physician, who took electrical measurements of Qiang's hands and ears and found "sensitivities vastly greater than [those associated with] modern military radar."

According to magician James Randi, Western conjurers have been reading with their armpits for centuries. Their technique is simple: They put one scrap of paper under an arm and hold another scrap in their hand. Wearing loose goggles instead of a tight blindfold, they discreetly peek down to read the message tucked in the palm, then deftly exchange it with the one in the armpit. Because they submit the scrap they have really looked at for examination, they always seem psychic.

Like these magicians, the sisters might be cheating. According to Cyrus Lee, of the psychology department at Edinboro State College in Pennsylvania, the Chinese experiments included scraps of paper handled freely by the girls, who used gogglelike blindfolds.

This man has been influenced against his will.

SUPER PAPER

Relax, this is not Super Paper. But if it were, you could be influenced against your will.

On the surface, Super Paper looks like plain white paper. But imprinted on it is a web of *invisible* suggestions that work subliminally on a person's unconscious mind. If you had to invite someone you hated to a party, you could print your invitation on Super Paper Type 2, which has hidden suggestions like *No! Don't Come!* Or if you wanted to see someone special, you could extend your invitation on Super Paper Type 1—*Yes! OK!*

How are the suggestions hidden? According to Super Paper inventor Derek Best, of Daytona Beach, Florida, the pattern of a woven finish is printed on plain paper with dark ink. Then words and phrases are printed over the dark ink in a lighter shade. The messages, written with letters about half an inch high, easily blend into the mesh of the fabric finish.

According to Best, the process works. His own career as a free-lance magazine writer, for example, has picked up significantly since he started writing to editors on Super Paper. "It won't make you jump up and act like a zombie," he says. "But it *is* persuasive."

Best now manufactures eleven types of Super Paper, including sheets that encourage people to buy a product, pay a debt, fall in love, or visit a friend. He has also developed adult Super Paper—with brand names such as French Lace and Black Leather—that contains "mature" suggestions. And he does custom orders.

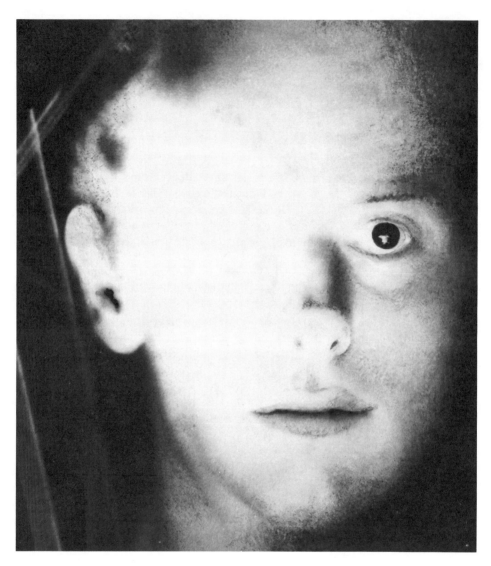

Inner human conflict may explain haunted houses, UFOs, putative apparitions, and bleeding statues.

"The number of ways for persons to occupy time is probably more unlimited than the number of ways in which matter occupies space."

—*Laszlo Moholy-Nagy*

HAUNTED PERSONALITIES

Haunted houses come into existence through the power of the human mind, says D. Scott Rogo, a Los Angeles researcher who's written several books on the subject. According to him, the personality of the main witness in many haunted houses is "basically hysterical, traumatized, and rather repressed. The repressed hostility erupts in a haunting, somewhat the way a kettle gives off steam," he says, and the result is mysterious poundings, flying objects, spontaneously ignited flames, even man-like ghosts.

Sometimes an act of violence, such as murder, will set up the psychic conditions that provoke strange sounds and visions, Rogo asserts. "When you talk to people in haunted houses, you often find there's a history of trauma in their lives. There do seem to be haunting-prone individuals."

Rogo, thirty-one, says that he lived in a haunted house in Los Angeles in the early 1970s. "I began to realize that you could feel when something was going to happen," he explains. "The house would act up and then die down for a few months. There were a lot of things I would previously have considered fantastical, but I knew they were real when I experienced them firsthand."

Rogo says his latest research indicates that inner human conflicts may account also for UFO abductions and putative apparitions. People who see bleeding statues, he remarks, have probably led traumatic lives.

DRACULA
REVISITED

You might take the precaution of packing a cross, a wooden stake, and some garlic for your vacation this year if you are going to be among the tourists joining a pilgrimage to Transylvania.

This annual tour, organized by the Dracula Society of Upper Upnor, England, is a two-week, thousand-mile journey that starts in Bucharest, where the sadistic real-life Prince Dracula ruled during the fifteenth century; the expedition later weaves through northern Transylvania, tracing the route of Jonathan Harker, the character who encountered Count Dracula in Bram Stoker's famous novel.

Bruce Wightman, tour leader and chairman of the Dracula Society, claims his intention is not to frighten people with the anticipation of encounters with blood-sucking vampires. Instead he wants his tourists to enjoy the trip on a romantic, scholarly, or humorous level. No one on the tour has ever been attacked by a vampire, Wightman adds, although one group was thoroughly unnerved by some mud-throwing gypsies, who objected to being photographed.

This year, Wightman says, there will be a special tour for Americans only.

PHANTOM ANIMALS

If at one time in your life you happen to see a few Australian kangaroos hopping down the streets of your neighborhood, and you see it every so often, you may be crazy. On the other hand, you may be actually witnessing a little-understood scientific anomaly commonly known as animal teleportation.

According to Loren Coleman of Boston, reports of animals mysteriously "teleported" from one location to another have been increasing for years. In 1980, for example, kangaroos were sighted in North Carolina, Oklahoma, and Utah. A penguin was found on the sand in Monmouth Beach, New Jersey. And several Florida residents said they saw six-feet-long Nile monitor lizards, native to Africa.

"The rational scientists would suggest that these were grown-up lizards brought into the States as babies," Coleman says. "But it's not that simple. There's a random pattern to these things; sometimes these animals literally come out of the blue."

Coleman, a school administrator and psychiatric social worker, has been studying teleported animals for twenty-two years. In that time, he says, he's tried to track down hundreds of mysterious animals through conversations with game wardens, police, and ordinary people. Usually, he admits, the animals' appearance can be accounted for. But 20 percent of the cases have remained total enigmas.

"No one has ever explained the mechanism for teleportation," Coleman notes. "Most of these animals have never even been caught. That's why we call them phantoms."

A boomerang-shaped UFO hovered over the Clifton,
Arizona, High School band.

HUGE UFO

It was the evening of October 23, 1980, and the Clifton, Arizona, High School band had gathered in the town stadium for its weekly rehearsal. The music surged and waned as parents and teachers watched from the bleachers. But suddenly the music stopped: The 150 people present saw a boomerang-shaped constellation of lights appear from out of nowhere.

"At first I found it hard to make the object out," recalls bandleader Bruce Allen, who guessed it was a plane. But once the brilliant boomerang had descended, filling "the entire stadium and maneuvering back and forth for about an hour, I grew certain it was nothing conventional."

Since then, area residents say, the UFO has made numerous visits to the Clifton area. Superior Court Judge Lloyd Fernandez, for instance, claims he saw the strange craft while taking an evening walk. In support of Allen's description, the judge noticed "six or seven lights in a distinct arrow shape."

And that same evening the alleged craft visited the home of Betty Jo and Don Sorrell. "I was trimming the Christmas tree when my husband yelled in that there was something strange in the sky," Betty Jo says. "I laughed it off, but when I heard a low humming, I went out. Sure enough, I saw it: steady red lights shaped like a boomerang, or a V. It circled the house four times."

According to Mrs. Sorrell, one rumor around Clifton had it that the UFO was probably an air tanker fueling jets. But she is skeptical. "It's like nothing we've ever seen out here. But I wasn't shocked or scared. After all, why assume the earth is the only place that has life?"

"The art of flying is yet in its
infancy, and it may hereafter
be brought to perfection,
and the time may come
when mankind may fly to
the moon."

—*Bernard de Fontenelle*

Victim of testicular feminization.

JOAN OF ARC: GENETIC MALE?

Joan of Arc fought bravely to free France from English domination. For her trouble a tribunal of French clergymen declared her a witch, and in 1431, at the age of nineteen, she was burned at the stake at Rouen.

Historical records dating from the time of the trial have convinced Georgia endocrinologist Robert Greenblatt that Joan had a rare syndrome known as testicular feminization. Caused by an enzyme deficiency, the syndrome prevents cells from receiving testosterone, the principal male hormone. "People with this condition look and think like females, but genetically they are males," Greenblatt explains. "Their testicles are up in the abdomen, just where the ovaries would be in a female. There is a normal vagina, but no uterus."

Greenblatt, who is writing a book about the love lives of famous people, learned from the testimony of witnesses at Joan's trial that she was a "well-breasted woman with a feminine, fruited voice" and that evidence of the "curse common to woman" was never seen on her clothes. He then discovered that midwives had examined her to learn whether she was a virgin. They told the tribunal that Joan was pure and that she had no pubic hair—a sign that she had not reached puberty.

"The excellent breast development, the failure to menstruate, and the absence of pubic hair are classic signs of testicular feminization," Greenblatt says.

> "Thousands of people
> are joining China's newest cult:
> a legion of witnesses
> with a fiery passion for UFOs."

UFO
UPDATE

Zhang Dengzhou was on sentry duty in China's remote Gansu province when he saw "an entire village enveloped in blue. I looked toward the source of light," Zhang reports, "and saw a flat, oval-shaped object, its center golden-yellow and surrounded by a deep orange cloud. After two minutes it picked up speed and flew to the east. The place was restored to darkness."

In America this tale might have been received with little fanfare, one UFO sighting among tens of thousands of others. But because Zhang was Chinese, his tale was special. A member of the highly respected People's Liberation Army (PLA), he had enormous credibility; nevertheless his fear of the authorities kept him from mentioning the story to anyone for at least a decade.

Recently many of Zhang's fellow PLA members have come forward to report UFO sightings as well. Their openness has inspired others: peasants, students, workers, teachers, even scientists. As China's repressive Cultural Revolution recedes, giving way to greater freedom of expression, thousands of people seem to be joining China's newest cult: a legion of witnesses with a passion for UFOs.

Nothing proves the earnestness of these amateur stargazers better, perhaps, than China's new *Journal of UFO Research.* Many of its reports, like Zhang's, come from the 1960s and 1970s, when talk of UFOs was considered "decadent and *bourgeois.*" Other accounts are more contemporary. Wang Tingyie, of Yunan province, for instance, reported a golden, cylinder-shaped object flying by his commune on April 12, 1981. And on December 21 of the same year, airport workers Wang Jian-jai and Han Feng-hsiang said they saw a "white disc suspended in the sky" high above the Peking airport.

These people and others, moreover, have begun discussing their pursuits through officially sanctioned UFO clubs all across the land. One of the country's most important groups ever was recently founded in Xinjiang province to analyze a spate of sightings along the Gobi Desert and the Soviet border.

Nonetheless UFO research in the People's Republic remains primarily a

UFOs over China.

spare-time activity that is pursued only by the novice. "The elite in the university departments of astronomy won't help us," complains one UFO buff who prefers to withhold his name. "They dismiss any discussion of extraterrestrial life as escapist Western thinking, and they have answers to explain just about every UFO sighting."

Even so, as Chinese leaders continue to emphasize free thought, UFOs may well gain wider acceptance. After all, the Chinese have always been among the world's most celestial people: They invented primitive rocketry, discovered heavenly bodies, and even developed an influential system of astrology. With more than a billion people looking skyward at night, China and her UFO watchers might soon have a lot to say.

"Perhaps you will say the
man is not young, I answer
he is rich; he is not gentle,
handsome, witty, brave,
good-humored, but he is rich,
rich, rich, rich."

—*Henry Fielding*

NUCLEAR
PREMONITIONS

In March 1979 a nuclear reactor at Three Mile Island in Pennsylvania broke down, spewing radioactive gas that endangered thousands of area residents. But, according to Larry Arnold, director of Harrisburg, Pennsylvania's Para Science International (PSI), the accident might have been prevented. Arnold conducted a door-to-door survey of Harrisburg residents and discovered that many people had been forewarned months before the accident.

"As many as thirty people experienced the same prophetic nightmare, in which they saw the cooling towers of Three Mile Island glowing deep red, with lightning crackling all around," Arnold says. He also claims that a woman who lives only seven miles from the atomic plant heard a news broadcast about the disaster one week before the accident.

To help avert future nuclear disasters, PSI has set up a national telephone hot line (the number is 717-236-0080). Should Arnold notice an inordinate number of psychic warnings from the area around a power plant, he'll alert the manager and request a shutdown.

The hot line has already yielded disturbing information: Three Mile Island is headed for another accident.

This woman has been damaged by Soviet rays.

ELF-WAVE ANTIDOTE

Soviet radar scans American airspace night and day, bombarding us with extremely low-frequency (ELF) radio waves. One Pentagon official, Lieutenant Colonel John B. Alexander, believes the Russians may be using these radio waves to manipulate our brain circuitry. His source of protection? A matchbook-size transmitter, called an ELF generator, made by a backyard inventor in Lakemount, Georgia.

Alexander, a former Green Beret, suggests that ELF waves short-circuit or jam our brain signals, leaving us susceptible to Soviet propaganda. "ELF waves won't make people run into the ocean on command," he says, "but they can degrade decision-making ability."

The ELF generator, Alexander says, is battery-powered. It emits its own ELF waves, which ostensibly interfere with Soviet transmissions. "The generator sets up a protective field. It is as if you had a little bubble around you," says Alexander, who wears the generator only when flying (it combats jet lag) and when forced to make crucial decisions.

Tape recorders may capture the sounds of our distraught, collective unconscious.

VOICES FROM BEYOND

Are odd sounds captured by tape recorders signals from the spiritual world around us? Sometimes but not usually, says William Braud, of the Mind Science Foundation.

Braud has found that many weird sounds are emitted by tapes that have been incompletely erased. Other strange noises result when a tape is made with one recorder, then played on another. Voices or music inadvertently recorded backwards on misaligned heads or crimped and folded tape can sometimes sound like bizarre wails and moans.

Yet Braud has also studied tapes with sounds that can't be explained as any of these things. Known among parapsychologists as "electronic voice phenomena," the otherworldly sounding tape recordings have been attributed to spirits, people from another dimension, and even the rumblings of our distraught, collective unconscious.

Braud says the Mind Science Foundation will continue to collect and examine unusual tapes at its center in San Antonio, Texas. "We're particularly interested in the possibility that some people may be psychokinetically imprinting the sounds," he says.

"We are in the early morning
of understanding our place
in the universe, and our
spectacular latent powers."

—Marilyn Fergenson

STAR
WAR

Astronomers used to believe that the galaxies were distributed more or less evenly through space, but lately they've found regions where galaxies are rare or absent. The granddaddy of these intergalactic holes, located near the constellation Bootes, measures more than 300 million light-years across—five times as large as its nearest competitor.

Asked by the *National Enquirer* to speculate about the void's origin, space shuttle engineer John Schuessler obligingly came up with a headline-worthy possibility: A fleet of intergalactic warships, each with the power to annihilate a solar system, might have attacked a rival supercivilization, setting off a chain reaction that could liquidate galaxies for megaparsecs around.

Even a less-than-super civilization could trigger such a cataclysm, he maintains. "We could destroy the earth with weapons now on the drawing board or already in our possession. That could upset the gravitational balance of the solar system, and the chain could go on from there. There's no telling how far the destruction might spread."

His scenario seems ripe for questioning. One of the void's discoverers, astronomer Paul Schechter of the Center for Astrophysics, asserts that the gap may not be truly vacant, just populated by galaxies too dim to be seen. And Schuessler himself speculates a real void could have emerged when a huge mass of antimatter was annihilated by the normal matter around it.

Yet these ideas depend on special conditions that may not have existed at the formation of the universe. Astronomers have yet to accept any of them. "It's pretty difficult to come up with an explanation more believable than interstellar war," Schuessler concludes. "I don't think we can rule that out."

LOVE MACHINE

Friends say William Waldron lost his job at Welldall Engineering, in England, because he fell in love with a computerized flame-cutting machine.

Yet Waldron claims this isn't *exactly* true: "I didn't love the machine," he says. "I just found it extremely interesting—futuristic, if you like. As a piece of machinery, it was fantastic."

Waldron explains: "Every morning before work I'd take the machine by the hand and program it to perform cutting maneuvers. When the machine moved, it was like watching my own brain."

But then the Welldall Company sent the machine to London for computer upgrading, and Waldron refused to work. "Despite our offer to let him operate the conventional machines," says Welldall financial director John Hinsley, "despite our promise to return the machine as soon as possible, Waldron stayed home for ten months without pay and was finally fired."

"Just call me stubborn," Waldron says. "But no other machine can take its place."

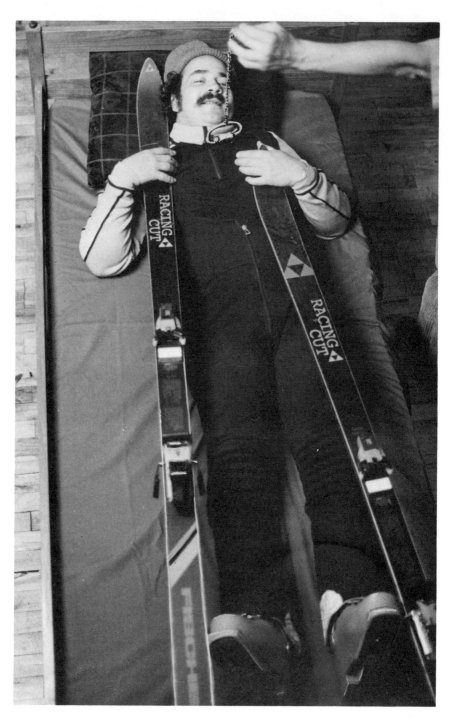

Was this man an alpine skier in a previous life?

"Man is so made that all his
true delight arises from
the contemplation of
mystery, and save by his
own frantic and invincible
folly mystery is never taken
from him; it rises within his
soul as a well of joy
unending."

—Vincent Starret

PAST-LIFE
SKIING

Gregory Paxson stood nervously atop a ski slope in Steamboat Springs, Colorado. It was his first time on skis, and friends expected him to fall. But as Paxson swept down the trail, his body twisted and turned with the smooth coordination of an expert. By the time his surprised friends caught up with him, he was in a state of exhilaration.

At the moment of push-off, Paxson explained, he experienced a sense of familiarity and then a vision: the dark, steep slopes of the European Alps. His first thought had been: *What a pleasure to be back on skis!*

Paxson spent the next eight years under hypnosis recalling prior incarnations. His conclusion? In one previous life he's been an Alpine skier.

Today Paxson is a professional hypnotist and past-life regression therapist in Chicago. In the last several years, he says, several of his clients have acquired skills learned during former incarnations. One man who remembered horseback riding in a previous life, for example, became an excellent rider. (Paxson admits that the man "supplemented the memory with horseback riding lessons.") Another patient, a practicing astrologer, recalled an astrology career spanning centuries. With the therapy, Paxson says, the man quadrupled his astrological skill in weeks.

Not all regressions, however, were helpful. Some participants rediscovered useless abilities, such as sundial reading and roof thatching.

> "Many of the
> drugs used to treat E.T.
> were destined
> for the cutting-room floor."

UFO
UPDATE

Back in 1982, a cute little creature named E.T., the Extra-Terrestrial, was accidentally marooned on Earth and almost died at the hands of a government medical team. Now a group of physicians are arguing over just where E.T.'s doctors—and director Steven Spielberg's off-screen medical consultants—went wrong.

For one thing, the doctors neglected to learn that E.T. had polished off a six-pack of beer, containing enough alcohol to induce severe hypoglycemia in a creature so small. Thus, say physicians Jonathan Wasserberger and Gary Ordog, of the Charles R. Drew School of Medicine in Los Angeles, they never administered glucose to correct a waning blood-sugar level.

Even more serious is a charge from Dr. Richard S. Weisman, director of the New York City Poison Control Center. E.T.'s constricted pupils and bluish skin were early signs of cyanosis, or oxygen deprivation, Weisman notes, and should have alerted E.T.'s physicians to the likelihood of a narcotic overdose.

E.T. was no junkie of course, but he was found by the physicians to be a mammal. All mammals produce morphinelike chemicals called endorphins, and E.T.'s body may have overproduced these natural opiates to compensate for the psychological trauma of being abandoned on Earth. The proper treatment, he adds, would be a narcotic antagonist like naloxone to block the action of the drug.

The doctors in Spielberg's film, on the other hand, administered only cardiopulmonary resuscitation, the standard treatment for heart attack. The technique does *not* include administration of glucose or naloxone. But Spielberg's chief advisor, Alexander R. Lampone, director of the emergency department at St. John's Hospital, in Santa Monica, California, did muster a defense. "E.T. received every drug known to our specialty in our resuscitation attempt," including glucose and naloxone, he wrote in a recent issue of the *Annals of Emergency Medicine.* "Unfortunately, many of the drugs used, the correct dosages administered, and the procedures performed on E.T. were destined for the cutting-room floor of the editing department."

Lampone also admits some uncertainty. "Please understand that we had no idea as to how our pharmacological agents would interact with E.T.'s photosynthesizing enzymes. And one look at his telescoping neck only confirmed our fears that inserting an esophageal tube would be difficult."

Despite the complexities, Weisman concludes, extraterrestrial patients resembling Earthlings can probably be given many current drugs without too much of a risk. If the alien is a truly unfamiliar life form, however, "we would try to follow basic cardiopulmonary resuscitation guidelines until new data were collected. But if the creature were in imminent danger, we'd have to treat it much like we treat Earth beings and hope for the best."

MUMMY'S
CURSE

Policeman George Labrash was guarding the treasures of King Tut in San Francisco's M. H. de Young Museum when he suffered a massive stroke. The attack occurred in 1979, but it wasn't until January 1982 that Labrash filed a suit claiming his illness was job-related. He was a victim of the dreaded mummy's curse, he said, offering as proof numerous deaths and illnesses allegedly caused by the mummy's wrath.

Deputy City Attorney Daniel Maguire, who was defending San Francisco against the pharaoh's vengeance, says he's unaware of any legal precedent for awarding compensation to the victims of curses. And a still healthy security guard, Richard Adamson, who actually *slept* in the tomb next to the mummy from 1923 to 1930, has recently said the story of the curse was deliberately planted to scare off would-be tomb robbers.

Apparently the San Francisco court agreed, for Labrash lost his suit. Now his supporters are urging him to have the case tried in Egypt.

"I do not think that the whole
of the Creation has been
staked on the one planet
where we live."

—*Sir Arthur Eddington*

INTEGRATRON

George Van Tassel built his extraordinary Integratron machine on 10.2 acres of land near Yucca Valley, California, in 1959. Head of the Ministry of Universal Wisdom, Van Tassel told his constituents he'd constructed the four-story dome according to blueprints sent by aliens from space. The Integratron would prevent aging and rejuvenate the old, he claimed, as soon as the extraterrestrials came to calibrate it. They never did. Unable to tap the machine's power, Van Tassel died in 1978.

Then, in 1979, Van Tassel's widow, Dorris, deeded the structure to the Christology Church, which in turn assigned it to Donald Lockwood, a mechanic in San Francisco. Dorris, who claims she signed the deed against her will, is now trying to reclaim the machine. But the courts recently issued an injunction preventing her from interfering with Lockwood's possession until all suits and countersuits have been settled.

Meanwhile Lockwood opened the Integratron's doors to the general public for the first time on April 24, during a two-day convention called SPACE (Star People Announcing Christ's Encounters) '82. Attendees were disappointed to find that the Integratron's seventy-five-foot diameter interior showed little evidence of high technology. Two doors on opposite sides of the dome led to a room with concrete floors, wooden walls, a tesla coil, and a rheostat.

Among the most disheartened were elderly members of the now-defunct Ministry of Universal Wisdom, who allegedly sent Van Tassel some $500,000 worth of social security checks each year in hopes of gaining immortality. Lockwood told them he would no longer accept their contributions, nor could he promise them eternal youth.

He added that he would be happy to hear from anyone—human or otherwise—who knows how to make the Integratron work.

Molecular biologists will redesign man on
the computer.

FREEMAN DYSON'S
FUTURE MAN

Imagine a noseless man with sealed lips and crocodile skin, a creature perfectly adapted for survival in the frozen vacuum of space. In the not too distant future genetic engineers may be able to sit down at computer consoles and type in the DNA codes for these and other beings designed to explore distant planets.

That's the vision of physicist Freeman Dyson, of the Institute for Advanced Studies in Princeton, New Jersey. "Nature's language for genetic instruction will be understood in ten to thirty years," he says. And molecular biologists have already begun developing the technology for redesigning Earth life to thrive in space or alien environments—without the need for spacesuits or artificial life-support systems.

For instance, the tendency of bones to dissolve during prolonged periods in zero gravity can be overcome, Dyson says, by readjusting the body's chemical balance. The frigid cold of space could be neutralized by endowing people with natural insulation. "Fur, feathers, nearly anything of this sort would do."

The most difficult problem might be the lack of atmospheric pressure, without which blood will begin to boil inside the body within five seconds. A possible solution, Dyson says, would be an internal body pressure a fraction of the one we have on Earth; the pressure would be contained by an airtight, reptilian skin and a special swallowing reflex to keep the body's fluids and gases from pouring out.

The nose, he says, could be dispensed with altogether. "There's nothing up there to smell anyway."

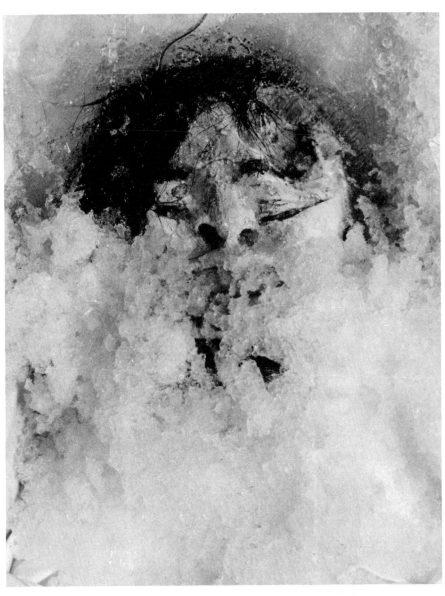

Frozen form: Is it the missing link or a
bashed-in rubber model?

MONSTER ON ICE

If you've shopped at malls on the East Coast, you might have seen a refrigerated coffin containing a hairy, humanlike body with a bashed-in skull. You probably also saw ads calling this grotesque creature "the missing link between man and the apes . . . still frozen in solid ice."

Promoter Frank Hanson has made his living exhibiting this "Big Foot Creature" at malls and carnivals for the past fifteen years. When someone asks how he got into the business, he might describe the Russian seal hunters who found the corpse floating in a 6,000-pound block of ice. The frozen corpse wound up in Hong Kong, where it was bought by the agent of an anonymous California millionaire, Hanson says; the millionaire later met Hanson and paid him handsomely to show the monster to the public. The dubious are shown a 1969 *Argosy* magazine story identifying the creature as a Neanderthal man frozen alive eons ago.

But when Hanson took his show to Providence, Rhode Island, in 1982, the Providence *Journal*'s science writer, C. Eugene Emery, decided to investigate. He eventually contacted Leonard C. Bessom, a retired paleontologist for the Los Angeles County Museum. Bessom said that in the early 1960s he was asked to make a model of a Cro-Magnon-type man that would be exhibited in ice; not wishing to tarnish the museum's credibility, however, he declined.

But he related that the creature *was* eventually built by Disneyland model maker Howard Ball. Ball is now dead, but his widow Helen and son Kenneth confirmed the story. Kenneth Ball, who helped his father make the creature out of rubber, said it was modeled after an artist's conception of a Cro-Magnon man. "We gave it a broken arm and a bashed-in skull, with one eye popped out," Ball volunteered. "The creature was the result of my dad's imagination."

When Jesus is reborn, he'll have enough money to buy a Jacuzzi and a condominium.

"He who does not fill his world with phantoms remains alone."

—Antonio Porchia

JESUS INSURANCE

Jesus was born on a bed of hay in a manger surrounded by farm animals approximately 2,000 years ago. When he is reborn, though, he'll have enough money to buy a Jacuzzi and a snazzy bachelor's condominium in Miami Beach.

The unexpected windfall comes from Ernest Digweed, who died six years ago, leaving Christ his entire estate. Digweed, of Portsmouth, England, believed Jesus would return to Earth in 1999. So he instructed the State Public Trustee Office to invest his money in government bonds at a rate of 12.5 percent interest, guaranteeing Jesus a total yield of $615,820 by the end of the century.

Digweed's distraught relatives are now contesting the will. Since the Trustee Office cannot break its agreement with Digweed, however, the family has decided to make an unusual arrangement: an insurance policy that would pay Jesus the lump sum of $615,820 upon his return.

Insurance broker Gess Fox says there seems to be just one problem: A couple of people masquerading as Jesus reborn have already staked claims to the cash.

Yugoslav clock: Can the time it keeps dilute the power of ESP?

TIME FOILS ESP

The marvelous, quintessential thing about ESP is that it seemingly knows no bounds, operating across all kinds of physical barriers and incredible distances. But proponents of extrasensory perception fear that this refusal to behave like other natural phenomena is what bars ESP from serious scientific consideration. If only ESP would decay over distance, like a sound wave, or yield to interference, like light from distant objects in space, physicists might be more accepting of it.

And so it was with mixed emotions that parapsychologist Charles Tart of the University of California at Davis, discovered that ESP is weakened by time. "This is a major surprise and could be a major breakthrough," Tart says, "because no one has yet found a physical correlate for ESP." He is hopeful that time, the physicists' fourth dimension, may be the bridge across which systematic study will flow.

Tart made his finding serendipitously while reviewing the most successful ESP experiments published since 1937. He was trying to discover what was going on whenever ESP was operating strongly and consistently.

"I noticed that not one of these experiments involved precognition," Tart reports. In other words, ESP never operated strongly or consistently when the target did not yet exist, as when subjects were asked, *before* a deck of cards was shuffled, to state what order the cards would be in afterward. When the intuited event has not yet occurred, Tart concludes, ESP may lose up to 90 percent of its strength.

ROACHSTER

The energy crisis has spawned electric cars, hydrogen cars, even wood-burning cars. But according to Thomas Easton, twenty-first-century man will find none of these as economical as the roachster—a living hybrid cloned from the lightning-quick cockroach and the hard-shelled lobster.

First, Easton explains, scientists will fuse cells from the cockroach and lobster. Then, after a bit of genetic engineering, they'll turn these tiny hybrids into twenty-foot-long roachsters, each with a large hollow wart that could function as a passenger compartment. Windshield, dashboard, radio, and upholstered seating would be built into the wart; headlights and bumpers would be bolted to the creature's shell. And the roachster's legs would rotate a set of wheels, propelling driver and passengers along at highway speed.

Drivers could steer or accelerate with electronic levers and buttons wired into the roachster's central nervous system, Easton suggests. Instead of turning off the roachster after pulling into a parking space, the driver would push a button to slow down the creature's metabolism and put it to sleep. And the roachster's antennae would serve as natural accident-avoidance sensors.

Easton, who teaches technical writing at the University of Maine in Bangor and has a Ph.D. in theoretical biology from the University of Chicago, envisions a mixture of alfalfa hay and high-protein supplements as a fuel source. But he still sees two major problems: Like the lobster of today, the roachster would periodically shed its shell. And like the horse, it would drop excrement all over the road.

"When we analyzed
the data, a relationship between
UFO sightings and
earthquakes jumped out at us."

UFO
UPDATE

UFOs are not necessarily exotic beings that come down from the sky. They might be powerful natural forces that come up from the earth. So claims Canadian scientist Michael A. Persinger, who believes that 85 percent of UFO sightings are nothing more than luminous electromagnetic-field effects produced at stress points along geological fault lines.

A psychologist and geophysicist at Ontario's Laurentian University, Persinger programmed a computer to correlate UFO reports with "high-energy natural phenomena such as earthquakes, hurricanes, tornadoes, and volcanic activity. The relationship between UFO reports and earthquakes," he says, "jumped right out at us."

The process begins, Persinger explains, when tectonic plates interlock, and immense pressure builds up, grinding quartz and other crystalline rocks in these regions for brief periods. The strain causes the atomic bonds in the rock to vaporize, creating a plasma resembling "a tiny piece of the sun."

"This luminosity, surrounded by an intense electromagnetic halo, rises to the surface and follows the local topography. People see these fields anywhere there is an electrical charge source—near church steeples, the tops of hills, near radio or television antennas."

Since the Curie brothers discovered the effect in 1880, scientists have known that crushing crystalline rock under great pressure creates an electromagnetic field. But without a computer, says Persinger, "no one could have correlated all the data pointing to a relationship between sighting luminosities and fault strain."

Studies of the phenomenon have been further complicated by a problem in our powers of observation, Persinger says. "Since our minds are sensitive to electromagnetic fields," he notes, "our ability to measure them is impaired. Sometimes energy generated at these geological stress points can produce seizures and hallucinations."

The kinds of alien life forms most often reported in UFO encounters

Crystalline rocks: Do they generate electromagnetic fields and induce hallucination?

"frequently resemble the distorted perceptions created when the brain is electrically stimulated during surgery," Persinger adds.

Some UFO field researchers, including those who supply Persinger with reports to aid his studies, question his theories. One asks, "Could the UFOs be using the electromagnetic fields along fault lines as guidance systems the way airplanes sometimes follow railroad tracks?"

Persinger rebuts: "I could say that all human neuroses are caused by invisible pink elephants pissing on us. That's hard to disprove, but it has limited value to a scientist. For hard-core proof, you need data."

Persinger, who has published maps showing the relationship between fault strain, earthquakes, and UFO sightings, believes he has the data. Could UFO reports near fault lines predict upcoming earthquakes? "That's what we're looking for," he enthuses. "And we think we have the evidence."

> "Space is felt as a great thing. There is some pinch of narrowness to us, and we laugh and leap to see the world, and what amplitudes it has . . . which yet are but lanes and crevices to the great Space in which the world swims."
>
> —*Ralph Waldo Emerson*

UFO COUNSELING

If you've had a "close encounter" with a UFO, you're probably confused. You might want to harbor such knowledge, but . . . you'll never forget the experience. Yet if you're like most people, you won't tell anyone about it. They'll think you're crazy.

Now, though, you have a place to go: the UFO Contact Center, in Seattle, Washington. "We help those contacted by UFOs to resume normal, decent lives," says Don Edwards, who runs the center with his wife, Aileen.

The center began operations in March 1981, after two previous attempts. Now it's going great guns, Edwards reports. The people who call or come by represent all ages and occupations, he adds, though a large number of them are either American Indian or Jewish.

These people, Edwards says, have great difficulty coping with their experiences. Like the character portrayed by Richard Dreyfuss in *Close Encounters of the Third Kind,* they find that "their families don't understand and their husbands or wives think they're out to lunch. We try to help them level out and reach a balance."

The center sponsors Saturday night drop-in meetings for close encounter victims to meet and share their experiences. For more information or for assistance, call 206-722-4655 or write to UFO Contact Center, 5723 South Bangor Street, Seattle, WA 98718.

BUBBLING
BLOOD

Each September and May thousands of Italians honoring the Christian saint Januarius flock to the cathedral of Naples. Most swarm outside the building, but one hundred fortunate souls are allowed inside, where they witness a group of elderly women mutter and shout at two small phials filled with a brown, crusty substance. That substance is alleged to be the blood of the saint, who was beheaded by the Roman Emperor Diocletian in A.D. 305. And the women, thought to be his "relatives," are cheering him on as his blood changes from gritty brown to a violent, bubbling scarlet.

Theologians and historians have debated the authenticity of this so-called blood for centuries, but it wasn't until 1902 that a group of *scientists* decided to investigate. Working from their lab at the University of Naples, the researchers passed pure white light through the material and found that emerging rays were virtually identical to those produced when light was passed through normal human blood. The scientists knew that *really* normal blood would have putrefied centuries ago, and they theorized that the sample had been contaminated by a foreign substance.

Then in 1950, University of Naples researcher Gastone Lambertini suggested taking a sample of the blood for chemical analysis. But church authorities prevented it, contending that if the blood were removed from the phials, it would disintegrate. This, according to Lambertini, remains a major stumbling block in solving the case.

Yet just recently writer David Guerdon says he's documented some more facts about the blood merely by looking at it: It bubbles no matter what the temperature within the cathedral, he reports, and it shows drastic changes in volume. The blood seems to pour from a central "ball," or clot, that remains crusty throughout the "miracle," Guerdon adds, and that same clot later absorbs the blood as it dries.

The church itself is noncommittal about the phenomenon. "It may not be a miracle," a spokesman said, "but whatever it is, it somehow functions outside the realm of ordinary laws."

"Wisdom is still a galaxy
light-years away."

—*Jack Henry Abbott*

HIEROGLYPHIC HOAX?

Imagine a not-so-fine spring day in 1477 B.C., near the point at which the Nile meets the Mediterranean. To the north, on the Greek island of Thera, an erupting volcano spews clouds of ash and sends a towering tidal wave toward Africa. To the south, the Israelites are escaping from Egypt, with Pharaoh Hatshepsut's troops at their heels. The Hebrews have just taken temporary refuge on a plateau when a flash flood caused by the wave washes over the desert below. In minutes it has wiped out the Egyptians and given the Israelites their freedom.

Thus, argues Hans Goedicke, chairman of Near Eastern Studies at Johns Hopkins University, is how the biblical story of Exodus *really* happened. Goedicke came up with this theory after retranslating hieroglyphics from a temple built during Hatshepsut's reign. His new translation, a ripping tale of wandering Asiatics and surges of primeval water, seems to conform to the Bible's Exodus story.

Front-page coverage of Goedicke's theory in the New York *Times* in May 1981 provoked author George Michanowsky, an expert on ancient astronomical texts, to cry foul. "Goedicke surreptitiously altered the hieroglyphic text and grossly mistranslated the key sequence," he asserts. "The definitive, authoritative text of that description was made by Sir Alan Gardiner years ago."

Saying he was tired of the whole debate, Goedicke refused to defend himself to *Omni*. Elsewhere, however, Goedicke has dismissed Michanowsky's accusations. He explains that he used legitimate techniques to "restore" some missing symbols and come up with the revised translation.

But other scholars agree that Goedicke's translation of the inscription is, as one put it, "all wet." Upon examining the hieroglyphics, University of North Carolina experts could find no specific reference to either water or Asiatics.

65

Pyramid home: When complete, it will contain Egyptian statues and hieroglyphics.

SUBURBAN PYRAMID

James Onan first read that pyramids could heal wounds, sharpen razors, even sap coffee of its bitterness, some fifteen years ago. Fascinated but skeptical, he soon set out to test pyramid power for himself.

Using his expertise as a building contractor, Onan first constructed several eight-inch-tall pyramids and passed his hand over each. One of the models, he says, zapped him with a jolt akin to a mild electric shock. He repeated the experiment several times, then had visitors try it too. Everyone said he felt the same sensation.

Onan went on to bigger and bigger versions, and now he is on the verge of completing his masterpiece—a six-story pyramid *home* on the outskirts of Gurnee, Illinois. A one-ninth scale model of the Great Pyramid of Cheops in Egypt, the wood-framed structure contains Egyptian statues and hieroglyphs. For security, it is surrounded by a moat, with dogs patrolling outside and a sphinx guarding the door. And, Onan says, over the next couple of years he will increase the pyramid's power tenfold by applying gold leaf to the entire outside surface.

Onan hopes that once he and his family move into the structure, they'll be able to conduct the first ongoing pyramid experiment in history. Yet Onan claims that the pyramid's power has already begun to show itself: A spring that started spontaneously right at the base of the pyramid, he claims, produces plant sprouts eight times faster than other water. And chickens drinking from the spring have grown 20 to 25 percent faster than chickens drinking elsewhere.

The Out-of-Body experience
is most common in those
who attend church.

"What are we here for?"

—*Calvin Coolidge*

OUT-OF-BODY SURVEY

Millions of Americans have journeyed to other worlds without their bodies or the use of spaceships, according to Kansas scientists studying the out-of-body experience (OBE).

Wondering whether reports of OBE's—the sensation that the "mind" is leaving the body—had any validity, psychiatrist Fowler Jones and two colleagues from the University of Kansas questioned 420 randomly selected people from 38 states and three foreign countries. The result? Of those interviewed, 339 had had at least one OBE, and some had had hundreds. Eighty-five percent of those who had OBE's said the experience was pleasant, while a mere 5 percent said they felt as if they were going crazy.

What exactly is taking place when people have out-of-body experiences? "All we can say at this point," Jones says, "is that people who have such experiences feel they're quite real. They describe them in various ways, but the common denominator is that the mind, the 'I' part of the personality, the thinking-feeling part, is no longer located inside the physical body but is deposited somewhere else in the environment. It is as if they have a mobile center of consciousness located just a few feet, or several miles, from the physical body."

Jones emphasizes that OBE's are experienced by healthy, intelligent people, many of whom attend church on a regular basis. The OBE is not the result of a drug-induced stupor, he says, nor is it merely a dream. If it were, he adds, it would be impossible to explain just why so many events glimpsed during an OBE turn out to have *actually* occurred.

One man interviewed in the study, Jones notes, felt that an OBE saved his life. His mind left his body and wound up in a room filled with coworkers plotting his death. After returning to his body, the man said, he confronted one of the conspirators and frightened her into admitting the grisly plan.

AMERICAN TRIANGLE

Just when you thought you already had enough to worry about, a new problem looms on the horizon: The dreaded Bermuda Triangle is moving toward the United States. That's the conclusion of Hugh Cochrane, author of *Gateway to Oblivion* and an authority on deadly triangles worldwide.

Cochrane says that there "definitely seems to be a westward shift" in the Bermuda Triangle, whose destructive force he attributes to energy that emanates from the bottom of the ocean. Triangle zones can move, he explains, much as earthquake zones do.

As a result of the shift, Cochrane says, Americans can expect to see a great increase in train wrecks and airplane crashes. Indeed some experts say triangle energy can already be found in the Great Lakes. Others contend that the peak of the triangle has moved to the treacherous Bay of Fundy, between Maine and Nova Scotia.

SEALAND

A huge steel platform rising out of the turbulent North Sea may soon become one of the most lucrative nations in Europe. This tiny kingdom, which goes by the name of Sealand, is located a mere sixty miles from London, but it has its own currency and stamps, an army, and even a heliport.

Sealand may sound like a fairy tale, but it has a real history: It began as a 140' × 40' fortress built by the British during World War II. After the war the platform was abandoned, and British millionaire Roy Bates started thinking he'd like to own it himself.

Plotting with his wife Joan and his son Michael, Bates invaded the fortress from a small boat fifteen years ago. When a British ship finally arrived for a showdown, Michael shot at its bow. The vessel sped away, and the real battle over Sealand was raged in the courtroom, where Bates came out triumphant. England had relinquished its legal right to the slab, the court decided, and it belonged to anyone who settled there. The "principality" of Sealand came into being officially in 1967—with the Bateses as its monarchs.

According to Joan, Britain was loath to cooperate with Sealand in the early days. But now, she says, "The English help us because they know we'll be a commercial asset." Indeed if the Bateses' vision materializes, calling Sealand a "commercial asset" would be putting it mildly. Michael says that engineers and a business group are now drawing up the final blueprints to turn Sealand into "the marketplace of Europe, a bureaucracy-free port similar to Hong Kong."

The Bateses plan to buy tons of cement and landfill to extend the island's boundaries dozens of miles. And they are seeking additional capital to build gambling casinos, an amusement park modeled after Disney World, an exclusive residential area, and Europe's largest gold and silver market.

> "How many of our daydreams would darken into nightmares if there seemed any danger of their coming true!"
>
> —*Logan Pearsall Smith*

LIVING NEANDERTHALS

What happened to Neanderthal man? According to one view, he was killed off in battles with modern man. Another theory has it that the Neanderthals—a relatively sophisticated, moral, and intelligent subspecies—mated with their *Homo sapiens* competitors, producing offspring that evolved into the European people of today.

Now there is yet another hypothesis: A respected archaeologist at Britain's University of Leicester proposes that small Neanderthal bands may still be alive and well in Outer Mongolia. After reviewing many Soviet reports of the Neanderthal-like wild man known as *Almas,* Myra Shackley concludes that "the idea that modern man can be the only surviving hominid species is outmoded biological arrogance. It seems impossible," she says, "to deny the existence of the *Almas.*"

According to Shackley, reports of the *Almas* have come from responsible citizens, including scientists, in the rugged, high mountainous areas of southern Russia and central Asia. Moreover, during fieldwork in Outer Mongolia, one of the most desolate places on Earth, Shackley herself found Neanderthal-looking stone tools. She crisscrossed the fringes of the Gobi Desert and the Altai Mountains, asking about the origins of the tools. Invariably, she relates, herders stated that they were made "by people who used to live in the area."

These people, the Mongolians told her, currently inhabit caves high in the mountains, where they hunt for food. The herders were surprised that anybody would be so interested in the cave dwellers, or *Almas,* Shackley says. "To the Mongols, they were common knowledge."

Most scientists will doubtless react negatively to Shackley's views, recently published in the prestigious archaeology journal *Antiquity*. Nevertheless Shackley proposes more fieldwork in Mongolia to find further archaeological remains—or perhaps the Neanderthals themselves.

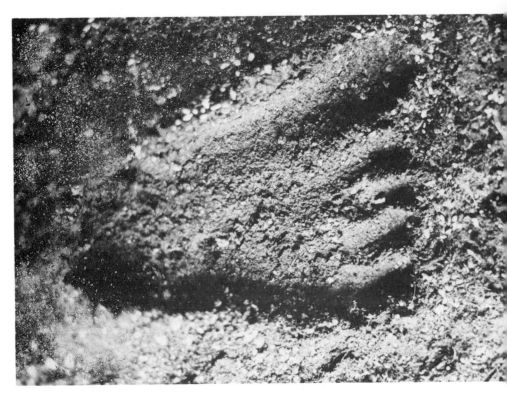

Phoney Bigfoot print: Hoaxers made prints like this one in Washington State.

BIGFOOT
FRAUD

For centuries Indians told of an apelike giant who roamed the forests near Mount St. Helens in Washington. The myth seemed to blend with reality when people started finding giant footprints in the late 1920s. But now an aging mountain man says the modern proof for the creature called Bigfoot is merely an elaborate fraud.

"I whittled those feet fifty-four years ago," says eighty-five-year-old Rant Mullens, a retired logger from Toledo, Washington. "It was just a practical joke."

Mullens says it all started in the late 1920s, when he thought he'd play a joke on some huckleberry pickers who occasionally visited the mountains. He whittled a couple of pieces of alder wood into fourteen-inch-long human feet with primitive heels and thick, blunt toes. A friend grabbed the feet by the poles they were attached to and walked around where the pickers would be. Mullens says, "When the pickers saw those huge footprints, they went running, all out of breath."

The Bigfoot tales might have died soon afterward, says Mullens, except that the joke soon got out of hand: Mullens stored the whittled feet in a logging shed, but a friend swiped them and carried on, leaving footprints throughout the country. Mullens regained the wooden feet in the late 1940s, but later he was enticed to sell them and six newly whittled pairs to a man from California. And so "proof" of Bigfoot, he confesses, spread throughout the Northwest.

Those who believe in Bigfoot say there is more evidence than Mullens' primitive footprints, including eyewitness sightings and candid films. But to Mullens the whole thing is "poppycock" spun off from his original fraud. "Anyone who believes in Bigfoot," he snaps, "has to be pretty narrow between the ears."

This corpse will deliver a message to the other side.

"Each man kills the thing he loves."

—*Oscar Wilde*

MESSAGES FOR THE DEAD

Men and women have whispered messages into the ears of the dying for thousands of years. If the terminally ill can somehow reach the afterlife, the age-old theory goes, they might be able to deliver messages to friends and relatives long since dead.

Now a Granada Hills, California, firm is capitalizing on this mystical communication. For a fee of forty dollars, Heaven's Union says, it can deliver a message of fifty words to the deceased by way of a terminally ill patient, or "messenger." According to company founder and president Gabe Gabor, the firm has already distributed 2,500 messages to fifteen ailing messengers. "Six of those messengers," he adds, "have recently departed."

Heaven's Union hires paradise-bound messengers through psychologists at hospitals, Gabor explains. And for each communication carried, the messenger's heirs are paid ten dollars. After the money has changed hands, the messengers simply read each message. They need not commit it to memory, Gabor says, because "when we leave our body behind, the spirit is able to recall all things from life."

Gabor's brainstorm for Heaven's Union came in the aftermath of his mother's death, when he instinctively asked a terminally ill friend to carry a message to her. "I know my mother received the message," he says, "because I have an inner feeling of peace."

As for criticism of Heaven's Union, Gabor says, "The greatest opposition comes from the clergy. They had a monopoly on heaven for years."

> "Would there be this eternal seeking if the found existed?"
>
> —*Antonio Porchia*

KAPLAN
ARCADE

Editor's note: Over the years *Omni* has covered the activities of Stephen Kaplan, the world's only vampirologist. Our stories on this unique researcher follow:

Fang Count, published in October 1981

Stephen Kaplan, of the Vampire Research Center, in New York City, has completed the world's first vampire census. The results? People in Massachusetts should worry.

After receiving more than five hundred responses, Kaplan found twenty-one vampires who "survive by drinking human blood" in the United States. For some reason, he says, U.S. vampires like Massachusetts best, with Arizona, California, New Jersey, and Virginia following in popularity. In addition he received scattered reports of cases in Canada and in countries as distant as Germany and Japan. Those who were enumerated in the census ranged from fifteen to forty-one years of "apparent" age, but some claimed to be as much as three hundred years old.

Some of the vampires who responded to the census do live in coffins but not underground. Kaplan himself asserts, "I never met a vampire I disliked. They're all fascinating . . . as long as they don't sup on my blood."

Vampire Hall of Fame, published in September 1982

Would you like to see the 1951 version of *The Thing*, a movie about a space carrot that sucks the blood of Arctic sled dogs? Have you been pestering bookstores for a copy of *The Hunger*, the tale of a gorgeous woman vampire who haunts New York City, seducing her meals?

If the answer to either of these questions is yes, you're in luck. A wealth of vampire-related arcana, ranging from Bram Stoker's fiction classic *Dracula* to the award-winning TV film *The Night Stalker*, will soon be available at the Vampire Hall of Fame in Queens. Under construction by Stephen Kaplan of

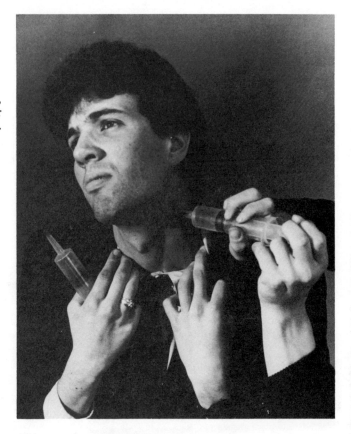

Vampires join fetish clubs, where they draw their blood with needles.

the Vampire Research Center, the new hall will keep the media and public informed about the new science of vampirology. "After a decade spent interviewing individuals who must drink human blood in order to sustain themselves," Kaplan says, "I feel it's time to share my findings with others."

Toward that end Kaplan has already stocked the Hall of Fame with manuscript copies of his own book, *Vampires Are.* A guide for those interested in becoming vampirologists, the book advises its readers against visiting a vampire alone. "For safety's sake the interviewers should outnumber the vampire subject substantially," Kaplan asserts, "but for the best defense I talk to them over the phone."

In addition to books and movies, the Hall of Fame will also contain photographs of ground-breaking researchers in the field. The only individuals thus far given this honor are Kaplan himself and his wife, Roxanne Salche Kaplan, an important member of his staff.

Vampirologist Goes Underground, published in May 1984

Dozens of cultists recently killed an unsuspecting victim and drank his blood. That, at least, is the claim of Stephen Kaplan, director of the Vampire Research Center in Queens, New York. "I informed the police," Kaplan says, "but they didn't get enough evidence to make an arrest, which means those sickies are out there looking to suck *my* blood for revenge. So I'm not just changing my voice, I'm going underground."

After thirteen years as a vampirologist, Kaplan says he will no longer interview bloodsuckers in the comfort of his home. Instead, he explains, he will change his address and conduct his research at a public meeting place like McDonald's under the protection of a bodyguard and a gun. He will also ask more questions to probe his subjects' mental health. "If a so-called Dracula tells me he turns into a bat," Kaplan explains, "then I know he's auditioning for the 'Gong Show.' He's a nut who might go for my throat."

Real vampires, Kaplan says, are just ordinary folk who happen to satisfy their daily nutritional requirements with blood. They don't live in coffins, and they don't have to suck blood from a person's neck. "Instead they join fetish clubs, where they draw one another's blood out with needles and drink it mixed with red wine.

"Unfortunately," says Kaplan, "in my business I meet more nuts than vampires. The followers of [rock musician] Ozzy Osborne have a vampire cult whose members draw blood through the body method, by ripping the flesh. I've fingered some of the group, but the others are sending me letters threatening to pluck out my eyeballs."

Though Kaplan is living in fear, "the police," he says, "just don't help. They think that a vampirologist is the same thing as a vampire and tell me I should be immune to death. But I ask you? Does a bacteriologist have to be a bacteria *[sic]*? I need protection. If anything happens to me, I'm going to miss myself."

Kaplan won't reveal his new address, but he *can* receive mail at P.O. Box 252, Elmhurst, New York, 11380.

An ancient corpse with shoulder-length hair was found in China.

BLOND MUMMY OF SINKIANG

A comely blond woman might not be so rare in Western societies, but what was she doing in China around 2000 B.C.? That's the question that's been tantalizing Chinese scientists since they unearthed a well-preserved Caucasian mummy in the northwestern province of Sinkiang.

Archaeologists unearthed the corpse while digging in the desert province near an atomic test site. According to a report in the *China Daily,* she's about five feet tall, forty years old, with reddish brown skin and blond shoulder-length hair. Her skin is still elastic because of the preserving qualities of the desert in which she was buried, and her internal organs are virtually intact.

Experts say she was probably a member of the Uighurs—forerunners of present-day Turks—who flourished as nomadic traders in central Asia centuries before Christ was born. Although the Chinese considered the Uighurs barbarians, Wu Tung, a curator at the Museum of Fine Arts in Boston, explains that these people possessed a rich culture influenced by Greeks, Chinese, and Indians alike.

Doctors in Shanghai who have been examining the mummy have found that her blood type was O, that she had high levels of cholesterol in her muscles and—inexplicably—the element antimony in her lungs. This mystery woman is certainly not the only Caucasian mummy ever found in China, but she *is* the oldest and most complete.

**Mysterious hitchhiker: A rare hallucinatory image
induced by the power of folklore?**

> "The supernatural is the
> natural not yet understood."
>
> —*Elbert Hubbard*

PHANTOM HITCHHIKER

Carpet-fitter Roy Fulton was driving home late after a darts match in Dunstable, England, when a gaunt, long-jawed man beside the road stuck his thumb out and hailed him. Fulton stopped the car, and the hitchhiker climbed in, clearly silhouetted in the overhead light triggered by the open door. The man said nothing, merely pointing straight ahead. So Fulton turned to the task of negotiating the car down the narrow road in the darkness. When he finally looked around to offer a cigarette, the man was gone.

Fulton's encounter with his disappearing passenger, parapsychologist Michael Goss reports, is only one of a rash of phantom-hitchhiker incidents in southern England in the past several years. Shortly after interviewing Fulton, Goss also visited the nearby village of Nunney, where a series of phantom-hitchhiker sightings had sent residents rushing to the local police in "virtual hysteria." And the same year Goss investigated newspaper accounts of one Maurice Goodenough, who had hit a girl hitchhiker with his car in 1974. Setting the girl beside the road, Goodenough had gone to fetch help, only to find the girl forever vanished when he returned.

In almost every instance Goss had trouble proving the truth of the stories. Newspaper accounts contradicted one another, few witnesses were named, and even when they were, Goss could rarely interview them. Fulton was the only "credible" witness he ever managed to find. After listening to Fulton's story twice one night in a Dunstable pub, Goss decided he was nothing more than a "sober, not overly imaginative working man."

Nonetheless the lack of witnesses who could corroborate Fulton's story or any other stories led Goss to doubt that phantom hitchhikers are physically real. Rather, he believes, they are a "rare hallucinatory event" brought about by folklore that lingers in our collective imagination from the time when man first drove horses and chariots. Late at night, exhausted and alone on a dark road, the vulnerable driver may summon the ancient hitchhiker from his unconscious; in his weakened state, he becomes convinced that the eerie fellow is truly sitting beside him.

BIGFOOT AT
WALLA WALLA...

To hear the Bigfoot fans tell it, it's finally happened: In and around the watershed area of Walla Walla, Washington, reliable witnesses have at last found tracks proving that an enormous two-legged primate stalks the American wilderness.

The watershed, a patch of mountainous woodland east of Walla Walla, provides most of that city's water. "Watershed riders" from the U.S. Forest Service patrol the area on horseback, ejecting would-be campers who might pollute the supply. And during one such mission, Patrolman Paul Freeman allegedly spotted a nine-foot-tall "Bigfoot."

Hastening back to the Forest Service post, he related the tale to his superiors, who mounted a search and found the first prints. They were fourteen inches long and pressed deep into the hard-packed dirt. A second trip into the wood produced nearly four hundred prints stretching for a mile.

According to John Beckjord, the Walla Walla finding is the first to give researchers some idea of what Bigfoot weighs. "The Forest Service cut out a footprint-shaped steel plate," he explains, "then backed a fire truck into it. The truck placed thirty-one hundred pounds of pressure on the plate, which dug a half-inch hole in the ground. The prints found by Freeman, however, were an inch deep—even more at the heel—so you know it took something really huge to make them."

Dennis Jones, Forest Service administrator for the watershed area, disagrees. "We called in an expert tracker from the border patrol," he reports. "From the placing of the prints, he was sure someone had made them deliberately.

"Paul Freeman was a real freak about Bigfoot," Jones adds. "He talked about it all the time. I don't know whether he made the prints or someone else did it as a practical joke on him. But we're sure it was a hoax."

Freeman, he notes, was an employee with the Forest Service for less than a month. He quit shortly after the would-be sighting and hasn't been seen since. Neither have the Bigfoot tracks.

"There are a few billion
planets, and among these a
few million no doubt have
civilizations more advanced
than our own. They will
have a different concept
of reality."

—*Arthur Koestler*

...AND
ON FILM

John Beckjord remains convinced that Bigfoot is real, however, and probably a lot stranger than any common ape. As proof, he cites the peculiar things he sees in the so-called Patterson film, a movie of a supposed Bigfoot taken by long-time monster hunter Roger Patterson in 1967 and rejected as a fraud even by many Bigfoot fans.

"I got a copy of the film," Beckjord says, "and enlarged it frame by frame. In one segment we have what looks like a long-legged female gorilla, with additional faces and little heads coming out of the main head, growing larger and then growing smaller and disappearing, like cactus buds. You're not supposed to see this sort of thing in traditional apes and men," he concludes. "It could be an alien."

So far Beckjord has convinced few of the dedicated people who search for explanations of Bigfoot sightings and other mysterious phenomena. "John's a wild and crazy guy," says Marcello Truzzi, head of the Center for the Study of Scientific Anomalies. "He's shown me his blowups, and there are smudges you might be able to interpret as he does. But it's like a Rorschach test. It doesn't prove anything."

Richard Greenwell, founder of the International Society of Cryptozoology, says, "We've rejected him for membership in the society, and he's been calling people all over the country and threatening to sue. If we have to, we'll accept him. But he'll be thrown out the next day."

Beckjord concedes that he has an image problem and not just photographically. "About half the people who've seen the enlargements agree there's something there," he sighs. "The rest think I'm some kind of nut."

MULTIPLE PSYCHIC
PERSONALITIES

People with multiple personalities have a lot to worry about: Possessing a number of separate identities that fight for control of their body. These identities usually aren't aware of one another, but when they are, the relationship is charged with hate. Now victims of this strange disorder may have to struggle with yet another problem. Some of the alternate personalities, says California psychiatrist Dr. Ralph Allison, wreak havoc with the help of psychic skills.

Allison, who devised his theory while treating dozens of split-personality patients, claims that "every one of them showed some evidence of psychic ability." In the simplest cases, he says, alternate personalities used psychic power merely to dominate the situation. Other times, though, the power seemed to come from a demon that had seized control of the body.

Allison says he concluded that demonic possession was often at the root of the illness when his sickest patients claimed to be "disincarnate entities." Shortly thereafter, he says, he began to notice that some of the alternate personalities couldn't possibly belong to the patients whose bodies they inhabited. One patient, Allison adds, was even controlled by the spirit of her boss's dead son. While psychotherapy had no effect on these spirits, Allison reports, they often disappeared after a brief exorcism.

But why should people who are suffering from multiple-personality disorders become possessed in the first place? "These people are like magnets," Allison explains. "The patient is full of hatred, and the personalities themselves call in the entities. They literally call for help."

Robots with sexual-service capabilities and humanlike skin may make ideal spouses.

ROBOT MARRIAGE

A sociologist predicts that there soon will be a new kind of mixed marriage: between human and robot.

"Man's capacity to manufacture a robot that appears and acts like a human is exponentially increasing," says Arthur Harkins, director of the graduate research program in futuristics at the University of Minnesota, in Minneapolis. "The advent of robots with sexual-service capabilities and simulated skin will create the potential for marriage between living and nonliving beings within the next twenty years."

Harkins suggests the domestic robots that first roll off the assembly line will be little more than sophisticated appliances, programmed to perform a small number of functions and to interact with humans in a limited capacity. But for very lonely people, these primitive robots will make excellent companions.

As artificial-intelligence systems are fully developed, perhaps with biologically based computer components, Harkins theorizes that robots (which don't age and can work nonstop) will become highly desirable as marriage partners for humans. In many instances, such marriages will be celebrated with traditional wedding vows and country-club receptions.

Eventually, Harkins believes, the robot will become the dominant being on Earth, capable of self-perpetuation through manufacture of new versions of itself. "Not all intelligent robots," he says, "will choose to consort with humans."

"Castles in the air are all right until we try to move into them."

—*Anonymous*

THE ALCHEMIST'S CURSE

Any self-respecting Renaissance king kept an alchemist or two at court. After all, with the alleged ability to change lead or mercury into gold, the alchemist was considered a hedge against royal economic disaster.

Such get-rich-quick notions were dismissed as utter nonsense by the nineteenth century, and today most scientists say alchemists were simply charlatans. There is one modern-day researcher, however, who disagrees. According to mineral economist and computer analyst Patrick Allen, of the U.S. Army, alchemists may have been transforming common metals into gold after all.

Early in the development of nuclear science, Allen explains, it was discovered that one element could be converted into another if it was bombarded with radiation. The radioactive energy would knock protons off the original element, transmuting it to a lighter substance with a lower atomic weight. Since mercury has only one more proton than gold, Allen notes, anyone with a powerful radioactive emitter could have performed the transformation with ease.

As it turns out, Allen says, ancient alchemists had access to a variety of emitters that could have done the job: Uranium and other radioactive ores were layered through the European mountains. And the alchemists themselves wore talismans made of radioactive fossils. Moreover, records left by medieval churchmen say that alchemists, doing the work of the devil, received divine retribution in the form of bleeding sores, racking pain, and nausea—all symptoms of radiation poisoning.

By the sixteenth century, alchemy was a vanishing art. But it may well be that, for a few hundred years at least, alchemists turned mercury to gold with the tools of nuclear physics.

The trauma of medical school is multiplied when deceased friends and relatives show up in the cadaver room.

FAMILY PRACTICE

With thousands of medical students dissecting thousands of cadavers each year, what are the chances of a student's finding the body of someone he or she knows? Better than you might think, according to some University of Alabama doctors who reported one such bizarre incident recently.

It happened on the first day of anatomy classes, according to a letter in the *Journal of the American Medical Association,* when a fresh group of medical students faced their first set of cadavers. Looking over the bodies, one female student was horrified to recognize her deceased great-aunt. The body, it seemed, had been shipped in from the state anatomical board in Florida, where the woman had died. Ironically the student had discussed the merits of body donation with her elderly relative some time before.

To their credit, doctors removed the body to another lab in the university and instituted a new policy of checking cadaver names with incoming students. "I was proud of the university for the sensitivity it showed," says psychiatrist Clarence McDanal, a co-signer of the letter. "That student," he adds, "quickly recovered from the trauma of the situation."

"Something
spectacular will happen
in 1982, and
Minnesota will be the place."

UFO
UPDATE

Leaving his companion Laverne Landis behind in his car, electrician Gerald Flach crawled off through the snowbound Minnesota pine forest. He managed to reach the highway, only to sprawl unconscious alongside the road. "We were waiting for a UFO," he mumbled to the incredulous motorist who found him. "I think my friend might be dead."

Flach's bizarre adventure began in June 1982. At the time he was vice president of a St. Paul, Minnesota, group called Search and Prove, whose members claimed to carry on telepathic discussions with aliens from space. Flach was sitting through a peaceful Search and Prove meeting when co-member Landis, a registered nurse, told him she'd heard from extraterrestrials who promised to save mankind—if she agreed to meet them in the wilderness for a ride aboard their ship. Landis asked Flach to join her, and he quickly agreed.

To meet up with the UFO, Landis said, they'd have to follow the aliens' instructions, no questions asked. Thus began their six-month journey. While Landis spewed instructions allegedly emanating from space, the two traveled to countless rendezvous sites throughout the Midwest and Canada. After months of dead-end instructions, Landis finally received what would be her last communique: Go to Minnesota's Loon Lake and stop eating.

The two made their way to the muddy shore, subsisting on vitamins and lake water for a month. Then, on the night of November 14, an unexpected snowstorm pounded their car. The battery died, and the vehicle could provide no heat to fend off the subzero temperatures. The couple began fading in and out of consciousness. "Don't worry," Landis would moan, "they won't let us die." But when Flach awoke, he looked down to see his friend's face puffy and blue. He made his way to the highway, where the helpful motorist found him and took him to nearby Cook County Hospital. There, Dr. Michael DeBevec broke the news: Landis *was* dead. She had succumbed to starvation and cold.

When asked to comment, Jerry Gross, president of Search and Prove, said that his friends' strange escapade was "truly miraculous." Gross claims that when the pair left town, "everyone just assumed that they were lovers and that they'd be back when they cooled off." But now Gross is convinced that Flach did meet up with aliens, learning enough to save humanity.

Back in St. Paul, however, some people say that Gross brainwashed the pair into going on their tragic mission. They believe that the group is a crazy cult and Gross a kind of Reverend Moon or Charles Manson. And they cite a 1978 article in the Minnesota *Dispatch.* "Something spectacular is going to happen in 1982," Gross is quoted as saying, "and Minnesota will be the place."

The mystery will go unsolved until Flach himself speaks up. But as a young boy who answered his home telephone put it, "We don't know where he is, and even if we did, we ain't telling *you.*"

"The divine art of miracles
is not an art of suspending
the pattern to which events
conform, but of feeding new
events into that pattern."

—*C. S. Lewis*

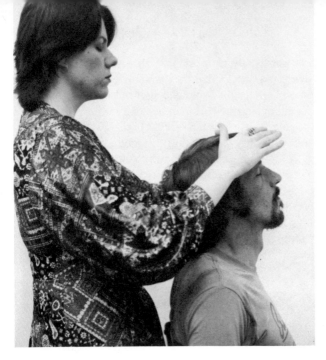

Miami physicians: They're starting to take the supernatural seriously.

PSYCHIC
M.D.'S

Medical schools may soon carry courses in a subject once laughed off as mere superstition—psychic phenomena.

In a survey of 228 medical-school faculty members, psychiatrist Stanley Dean, of the University of Miami in Florida, found that doctors are starting to take the supernatural quite seriously. Of the academics questioned, 58 percent favor the study of psychic phenomena in university psychiatric programs, 42 percent believe it's possible that paranormal episodes occur, and 35 percent claim either to have experienced firsthand a psychic event—such as telepathy, precognition, or altered states of consciousness—or to know someone who had.

Dean also says that many of the doctors surveyed believe psychic factors are important and see the need for research on healing by nonmedical means. Dean himself hopes to pursue "metapsychiatry," the study of the relationship between medicine and the paranormal.

"My colleagues are gradually coming out of the closet on psychic phenomena," Dean concludes. "More than half the sick people in the world seek out healers rather than doctors, and it's important to know why."

> "Something unknown to our
> understanding is visiting
> the Earth."
>
> —*Mitrovan Zverev,*
> *Soviet scientist*

UFO MUSEUM

What has four extraterrestrials, a mysterious talisman from somewhere in the cosmos, and reams of UFO footage? The World's Largest UFO Exhibit, on the fifty-first floor of the IDS Tower, overlooking the city of Minneapolis.

The five-room exhibit is stocked with mementos of close encounters: "authenticated" UFO photos; astronaut Gordon Cooper, on videotape, describing his UFO sighting; and tape recordings of people who have seen aliens peering in their bedroom windows and scurrying across their roofs. Some 250,000 visitors flock to the exhibit each year, eager to examine Jimmy Carter's report of a UFO sighting or try their hands at one of five "cosmic quizzes." ("What's the greatest number of people to view a UFO with occupants?" one display board asks. The answer: "Thirty-eight.")

"It's close encounters of the third kind—face-to-face meetings with aliens—that fascinate people most," says businessman Dick Hobson, founder of the exhibit. "If only we had an extraterrestrial walking around in here, we'd have lines fifty miles long."

Without access to any bona fide extraterrestrials, however, Hobson manages to attract crowds by inviting guest speakers such as J. Allen Hynek, director of the Center for UFO Studies in Evanston, Illinois. The exhibit is so popular that spinoffs have been launched in Sonora and San Bernardino, California, and a traveling version of the show may hit the college circuit soon.

A candle sparked the powers of a California psychic.

PSYCHIC GOLD

Like most people, Jake Rotstain wanted to get rich quick. So he advertised in the Kansas City *Star* for a psychic. If he could just get hired as a public-relations agent for a gifted seer, he reasoned, he'd make millions on TV and books.

The would-be entrepreneur placed his ad in the paper once a week for twenty years. Then it happened. On November 30, 1977, Rotstain claims, he struck psychic gold; he received a call from Lane Starkey, a twenty-two-year-old Kansas City art student with "extraordinary psychic skills."

According to Rotstain, Starkey met him for a chat that very week. "While I sat in my attic, staring at a candle," he related, "Starkey was locked in my basement. He drew that very same candle in a notebook as if he could see through walls right into my head."

Nevertheless Rotstain, a retired home-improvement contractor, has yet to cash in. Young Lane Starkey grew tired of waiting for his fortune and went off to art school in London. And Rotstain says he hears from him only now and then through the mail.

The Kansas City P.R. agent blames his misfortune on the Committee for the Scientific Investigation of Claims of the Paranormal (CSICOP). Since CSICOP's members include distinguished scientists like B. F. Skinner and Carl Sagan, Rotstain says, it has the power to test and legitimize those who claim to be psychic; in fact, without CSICOP's stamp of approval, book and TV investors won't take a psychic seriously. "Yet CSICOP has refused to test Starkey," Rotstain charges. "And the reason is plain. They know I'll make a billion, and they won't get a dime."

But according to CSICOP's president, Paul Kurtz, "that's just not true." On more than one occasion, he says, CSICOP offered to test Starkey. But whenever a date was set, Rotstain backed out. Consequently Kurtz now doubts that Starkey even exists. If Starkey is so talented, Kurtz wonders, why doesn't he agree to a test? Why doesn't he call CSICOP himself?

Part of the reason, Rotstain says, is that "Starkey's a mental cripple. He was jogging in London recently, for instance, and he ran smack into a stone wall."

CHESSIE
ON TAPE

The dining room of Bob and Karen Frew's Maryland home faces Chesapeake Bay. On the evening of May 31, 1982, with the sun still shining brightly, the Frews and several dinner guests noticed a dark object rise out of the water: It looked like a thirty-foot-long serpent punctuated with humps. Bob grabbed his video camera and began filming what he thought might be "Chessie," a sea creature that allegedly inhabits the bay.

A group of scientists from the Smithsonian Institution met with Frew and the other eyewitnesses to review the three-minute tape a few days later. George Zug, head of the department of vertebrate zoology at the Smithsonian's National Museum of Natural History, in Washington, D.C., says the film was "most interesting," but he refuses to speculate on what the object might be. He points out that the usual explanations for such "creatures"—partially submerged logs, for instance, or optical illusions—do not fit the elongated, animate object on Frew's film. He also states that the front end of the "thing" appears and disappears vertically on the film; it doesn't roll above and below the surface, as swimming animals would do.

The next step in the "Chessie" investigation is photo enhancement of Frew's film with a computer at Johns Hopkins University. In the meantime Mike Frizzelle and Bob Lazzara, of Enigma, a Maryland-based organization that investigates unexplained phenomena, are compiling a comparative study of past "Chessie" sightings—and any new ones that are reported. "We hope we'll be able to develop a pattern," says Lazzara. "We need to find environmental data common to most sightings, so we can go out and look for the animal."

"We didn't take 'Chessie' so seriously before," Frizzelle adds. "But the Frew tape elevated it from just folklore to a legitimate phenomenon—something to be seriously scrutinized."

"Striking Metro-North
trainmen saw the spectacular
lights hover over
their picket line in Brewster."

UFO
UPDATE

Meteorologist Bill Hele was cruising the Taconic State Parkway in Westchester County, New York, when he saw a checkmark-shaped object with six prismatic lights. The row of multicolored lights blinked off for a moment, Hele recalls, then shifted to brilliant green. The whirling form was almost a thousand yards across, he adds, and hovered a thousand feet in the air. Two or three minutes later it gradually drifted to the north and out of view.

So began the most spectacular display of UFOs in the history of New York State and possibly of the nation. On three consecutive Thursday nights as well as a couple of Friday and Saturday nights, from March 17 through March 31, 1983, hundreds of people around Westchester reported a boomerang-shaped object that hovered soundlessly and shot dazzling rays of light.

Within days of the first sighting, accounts were appearing in newspapers throughout the country. And the mounting reports soon reached Phil Imbrogno, a Westchester science teacher and field investigator with the Center for UFO Studies, based in Evanston, Illinois. Imbrogno, co-investigator George Lesnick, and J. Allen Hynek, director of the center, quickly launched an in-depth investigation, interviewing witnesses and cross-matching data with an Apple II computer. Doctors, lawyers, nurses, heads of corporations, and housewives, the team found, all gave descriptions that matched Hele's. Even a group of striking Metro-North trainmen were startled to see the spectacular lights over their picket line in Brewster.

The saucer-investigation squad also came up with some bizarre contradictions. Simultaneous sightings in towns miles apart suggested the presence of more than one object. And hundreds of sightings in five Connecticut towns a month after the Westchester incidents indicated a possible hoax. Witnesses there described engine sounds and maneuvers that could have been performed by a formation of small planes trying to mimic the original open V. Such reports, in fact, convinced one local Federal Aviation Administration official that a group of top-notch pilots flying out of the tiny Stormville airport, in Dutchess County, New York, had manufactured the flowing UFO.

But Imbrogno disagrees. "Single-engine planes," he says, "cannot hover soundlessly, make ninety-degree turns, or shoot down dazzling beams of light."

As for Hynek, he says the case is one of the most unusual he's ever seen. "Most UFO sightings occur on lonely back roads in places like Oklahoma," he notes, "but this UFO was seen in a relatively urban area over a number of days, with a broad spectrum of witnesses."

Well-known UFO critic and aerospace journalist Philip J. Klass also ventured an opinion: "I've been investigating UFO reports for seventeen years," he commented, "and have yet to find an indication of an unknown or extraterrestrial phenomenon. It would take a lot to convince me, but it could be that for the first time in seventeen years this is an unexplainable case."

There are only ten audio tapes in all of UFO recording history.

LOUD UFO

On the night of June 22, 1972, Javier Bosque, a seminary student in Logrono, Spain, sat in bed reading. It was nearly 2 A.M., and the local radio station had gone off the air. Suddenly, Bosque claimed, the windows swung open and a silver oval two feet in diameter floated in, flooding the room with light. Then the radio let out a bleating cry. Bosque fumbled for the cassette recorder stowed near his bed and quickly flicked it on.

It didn't take long for news of the resulting tape, one of only ten in UFO recording history, to reach Willy Smith, a retired nuclear physicist living in Norcross, Georgia. The eight-minute recording so fascinated him, in fact, that he analyzed it on his oscilloscope. By transforming the noise into visual images on a screen, Smith says, the oscilloscope made one thing perfectly clear: The sound waves somehow had jumped from a medium pitch, or frequency, of 420 cycles per second to a scream of 4,000 cycles per second.

"The skeptics," Smith says, "were dumbfounded. They obviously realized that only the most sophisticated and expensive equipment could produce a sound like that. It's not the sort of thing a seminary student in rural Spain would even attempt to fake."

But acoustics engineer Howard Schecter, who recently analyzed the tape for the Center for UFO Studies in Evanston, Illinois, says, "That's baloney! I could produce the same sound right now with simple electronic equipment. Besides," he notes, "analyzing such extreme fluctuations on an oscilloscope is like looking at DNA with a magnifying glass."

"The only test that could provide real evidence," Schecter adds, "requires a computer and thousands of dollars—money that ufologists just don't have."

Where does Javier Bosque fit into all this? He was last seen in a little village in the Spanish mountains. When questioned about the noisy UFO, he made it clear he had loftier concerns. "Leave me alone," he insisted. "I'm a priest."

Electromagnetic aura: Can it be enhanced by a special mouthpiece?

MAGIC MOUTHPIECE

If the muscles in your arms are turning to consommé, the problem may be your mouth. So says Dr. Richard Kaufman, an Oceanside, New York, orthodontist, who designed mouthpieces for Olympic and professional athletes. Kaufman and a few peers believe that by correcting the alignment of the upper and lower jaw, the mouthguard (dubbed MORA, or mandibular orthopedic repositioning appliance) can also boost an athlete's strength and energy.

This claim has provoked guffaws among other orthodontists, but Kaufman says he's found some new proof. A special "Kirlian camera," capable of photographing the body's electromagnetic "aura," he contends, has shown that MORAs actually do increase vitality.

In a recent study conducted in the kitchen of Pip Merrick, program director of the International Kirlian Society, Kaufman ran subjects through an arm-strength test while Merrick sat at the camera's controls. First with the MORA, then without it, each subject held an arm out at his or her side while Kaufman tried his best to push the arm downward. Meanwhile Merrick placed the fingers of the subject's other arm atop photosensitive paper. Turning the kitchen lights out, she then pushed a button and ignited a flat metal electrode beneath the paper. By exposing the paper to intense light, the electrode produced a photo of the aura around the fingers.

As far as Kaufman is concerned, the test proved that subjects wearing a mouthpiece were stronger and healthier. The reason: Their auras were fuller than the auras of those without the mouthguard. Merrick, however, feels he's jumping the gun. True, the subjects fended off Kaufman's downward thrust better when their jaws were properly aligned, but since they knew the aim of the experiment, perhaps they were only making him happy. And, Merrick says, even dedicated Kirlians would be hesitant to call a fuller aura a sign of physical health or strength.

"No man will be found in
whose mind airy notions do
not sometimes tyrannize,
and force him to hope or fear
beyond the limits of sober
probability."

—Samuel Johnson

Plants might help you communicate with the dead.

RADIO
FOR THE DEAD

If you've longed to contact the dead, here's some news that should interest you: Two-way conversation with the "other side" has reportedly taken place via Spiricom Mark IV, a ham radio system used for supernatural communication.

"We hit the jackpot on April 16, 1980," says Spiricom inventor George Meek, seventy-two, an air-conditioning expert and president of North Carolina's Metascience Foundation. He claims on that date to have contacted the spirit of George J. Mueller, a physicist who was employed as a professor at Orange Coast College in California before his death in 1967. "Dr. Mueller told us his social security number and intimate details of his life and scholastic activities—which we verified," Meek reports. Communication with Mueller suddenly ceased last November, however, and Meek speculates that the departed academic ascended to a higher astral plane, beyond Spiricom's range.

Spiricom, essentially a radio receiver that works at ultrahigh frequency, is operated by Metascience Foundation technician William O'Neill, who says he can see and hear the dead. Incoming spirit transmissions, Meek explains, travel from the receiver through an audio unit, which produces the robotlike voice of the deceased. "The entire Spiricom system, including the clairvoyant operator," Meek theorizes, "interacts with the space-time sector in which spirits like Dr. Mueller live."

The Metascience Foundation recently stopped testing Spiricom to focus on the use of plants as mediums for communicating with dead persons. But a cassette recording of Dr. Mueller's voice and a manual describing Spiricom can be purchased by writing to Metascience Foundation, P.O. Box 747, Franklin, NC 28734.

Carp fish: The key to immortality or the butt of a joke?

ELIXIR OF LIFE

Nature magazine, the most respected science journal in England, billed it as a breakthrough in antiaging research. A tiny protein named longevin, the publication reported, had been isolated in a carp by a Professor Obispo, of the Stoyte Institute of Life Sciences at Tarzana College in California. Longevin appeared to be responsible for the remarkable longevity of carp, which reputedly live to a ripe old age of 150, *Nature* said. Moreover, the tiny protein significantly prolonged the life span of mice as well. Similar treatment of humans, the writer implied in his article, titled "The Elixir of Life," could be just years away.

The difficulty arose when *Nature* readers attempted to track down both Professor Obispo and the science journals that had supposedly published the preliminary findings of his research.

When reached at his London office, John Maddox, the editor of *Nature,* promptly confessed that the article on longevin had been an April Fool's Day joke. "It was very unusual for April first to fall on a Thursday, our weekly issue date," Maddox confided. "And it was too good an opportunity to pass up. It takes very little in the way of general knowledge to see it was a joke. Since then we have received half a dozen articles in the same vein, obviously sent by scientists who accepted the joke in the spirit it was written."

When advised that the longevin article was now logged in the scientific data base and would be cited as a reference by other scientists, Maddox said, "I doubt it."

He'd better tell that to the researchers who put their faith in Scisearch and a variety of other computer banks now broadcasting news of longevin throughout the world.

SMALL
PEOPLE

Worried about the population explosion? Calm down. The burgeoning birthrate will cease to be a problem once we've bred a race of humans half normal size. That at least is the prediction of Thomas Easton, a theoretical biologist and technical writing teacher at the University of Maine.

"Cut people down to about three feet in height and they won't eat as much food," Easton says. "Cars could then be the size of little red wagons, with all the old gas guzzlers converted to buses. In fact man's appetite for open space and raw materials would decrease to match his stature.

"This new breed of human," Easton says, "would have far more muscle, with the ability to run and jump almost like a cat. Reduced weight would ease the wear in joints, cutting the prevalence of arthritis. Since less blood would be pumped through a smaller circulatory system, the heart's work load would be diminished and there would be fewer cardiac arrests.

"The technology to shrink humans," Easton says, "will probably be available within a decade. A genetically engineered virus, carrying genes coded to create small people, could be placed in a reservoir or released in the air. Then everyone infected would absorb the genes and produce lilliputian offspring."

But economist Anthony Wiener says Easton's forecast is ridiculous. "In the real world," he contends, "you deal with the population problem by reducing the birthrate. I expect countries with a crowding problem to legislate mandatory sterilization by the year 2000."

> "Intelligent aliens
> will stand upright, building
> their world with two
> arms and two grasping hands."

UFO UPDATE

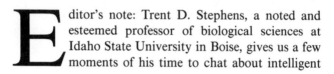

Editor's note: Trent D. Stephens, a noted and esteemed professor of biological sciences at Idaho State University in Boise, gives us a few moments of his time to chat about intelligent extraterrestrial life.

When Christopher Columbus first set foot in the New World, he was astounded at the sight of Indians. The great thinkers of his time, after all, had predicted a place peopled by monstrous creatures in no way human.

Modern scientists are now making similar predictions about worlds yet to be discovered in the vastness of space. The probability of encountering beings that are physically similar to us, Carl Sagan and others suggest, is near zero. Evolution, they contend, is a random process that must create radically different creatures from one planet to the next.

As a biologist studying the evolution and development of shape, I've reached the opposite conclusion: I am convinced that evolution follows stringent rules that would operate the same way on any planet in the cosmos. If that's true, we may be in for the same surprise as Columbus. Once again, somewhere in space, we may come face to face with ourselves.

My argument begins with simple biochemistry. For life to exist, chemical reactions must occur rapidly, and that's impossible without a liquid solvent such as water. But if water is to keep its liquid form, it must remain at once too cool to vaporize yet too warm to freeze. That's a tall order, and the only thing that can fill it is an Earthlike planet.

Most experts agree that the evolution of earthly intelligence is rooted in the primate's upright posture, which freed the hands for grasping and holding. Versatile hands allowed protohumans to use tools and fire, thereby stimulating the brain; that in turn led to more advanced technology, which further increased intelligence, and so on, until *Homo sapiens* evolved.

As far as I'm concerned, technology is essential to the development of intelligence, no matter what the planet. But if you're discussing an Earthlike world, then technology can be developed only by creatures just about the size and shape of human beings.

To sustain a fire, for instance, one must feed it fuel. This requires humanoid arms and legs to fetch the logs. It also means human size and strength to support the wood as it is toted from one spot to another. (A small creature on a world with Earthlike gravity couldn't carry logs large enough to keep the fire burning. An extremely large individual might lose its balance, succumbing to the force of a single fall.) And because brainy, bipedal extraterrestrials would actively pursue their food, their nose, ears, and mouth would be concentrated together at a leading end, allowing them to see, smell, breathe, and eat at once. The combination would form a recognizable face.

When we finally meet the extraterrestrials, the biggest problem will *not* be trying to figure out whether our strange friends are intelligent. Instead, the hitch might be convincing folks back home that the guests we have brought along with us really are aliens and not Leonard Nimoy or Christopher Reeve.

Malodorous vagrant: Some Californians have mistaken this hairy bum for a Bigfoot-like vagrant.

BUENA FOOT

In Los Angeles they sing of Buena Foot, a giant malodorous creature that haunts the city with menacing howls. Or at least he howled menacingly one recent May night, when people saw him in a Buena Park flood-control canal.

Over the next several days researchers from Special Forces Investigations, dedicated to the study of the paranormal, the monstrous, and the extraterrestrial, combed the area with divining rods and ventured 125 feet inside a concrete storm drain in hopes of finding the critter. All they discovered, however, were several four-fingered handprints, which they promptly copied in plaster casts for ongoing examination. They opined that the prints were made by a heavy, huge-thumbed creature larger and stronger than a man. The evidence fanned excitement and brought throngs of onlookers to the area. But it seems that Buena Foot himself was frightened off, for no one has been able to find a trace of him since.

The police, who joined the search grudgingly, were satisfied that the monster was really a hairy vagrant who slept in the park and howled for reasons of his own. They released a photo of the man, who, they said, matched Buena Foot's description "on at least seven points." But Dennis Ruminer, of Special Forces, declared the tramp was too short (only five feet, eight inches tall) to be Buena Foot, and he said that he and his team would continue their intensive search in Orange County, south of Los Angeles.

Meanwhile another bellowing vagrant was observed by independent investigator John De Herrera. This one was reported to be in his mid-thirties and just about six-feet-four.

Passion candles and rose-petal incense:
They attracted only losers.

"If a man die/it is because death/has first/possessed his imagination."

—*William Carlos Williams*

LOVE POTION

Singles bars and boring computer dates got you down? Barbara MacKay, an unemployed secretary turned stand-up comic, felt that way, so she bought a candle-and-incense ritual kit from the Mystic Eye occult shop in San Francisco.

MacKay cast her first love spell at home. She took a bath, dried off in the air without any towel, then anointed herself with evil-smelling oil. Finally she burned some pink "passion" candles and rose-petal incense while chanting her wish for a man.

The result, she says, was hard to interpret. "I met a lot of men almost immediately. But I had gone on a trip with Club Med. So I can't be sure how much the magic helped."

After a subsequent dry spell, though, she decided to try the ritual again. The outcome? One cable-car confrontation with a derelict, one cocktail with her downstairs neighbor, and three months of going-nowhere dates with a man she met at a local disco. Better than she'd been doing, but not much to show for an incantation meant to bring true romantic love.

"It was very painful for me," she notes, "but I can't blame the occult. It brought men, but finding the right one and making the relationship work was up to me."

MacKay's occult experience nevertheless was hardly a loss. After four rear-end collisions with her little Toyota, she bought some magic herbs for the floorboard and hasn't had an accident since.

LEAF
MONSTER

The renowned, much-sought-after, and frequently sighted monster of Loch Ness, affectionately known as Nessie, is not just one creature—and actually is not a creature at all—according to naturalist Ben Seniscal, of Buckinghamshire, England. Nessie, he declares, is merely an occasional heap of rotting leaves ripped from the bottom of the loch and propelled across its surface by the gases of decay.

Seniscal, who has worked for the Forestry Commission in Scotland, was knee-deep in the hippopotamus pond at the Whipsnade Zoo one summer day after its usual inhabitants had been absent for several weeks. Suddenly, he recalls, a large swirl of hippo droppings rose from the bottom of the pond, quickly gathered speed, and charged some seventy-five feet along the water's surface before gently sinking into the abyss. It was an important moment for Seniscal, who wasted no time in fitting the sequence of events to the area of Loch Ness.

Instead of the droppings that made up the pond monster, he contends, Nessie consists primarily of leaves from birch, oak, and other deciduous trees that account for the magnificent fall foliage around Loch Ness. Seniscal hypothesizes that some leaves and branches fall directly into the loch in autumn, while many more are carried there by the fast-flowing rivers and streams that feed into it. Like sleeping monsters, enormous mounds of various shapes remain quiescent under the pressure of the loch's waters all winter long. Then the warming waters of spring hasten decomposition, and the methane gas released by that process loosens rafts of sunken vegetation weighing tons.

Seniscal notes that television films of the monster show it traveling in a straight line only. Propelled by methane, he adds, his "monsters" would usually swim as the crow flies, too.

The theory suggests why Nessie has as many differently shaped heads as there are pictures of her: Her "head" must be a root or branch from a tree. The fact that she is most often sighted in July or August is also consonant with Seniscal's idea. And of course reports of Nessie's strange silence—rarely more than a gurgle as she vanishes—are easily explained by the leaf hypothesis.

How to prove the true nature of Nessie? "One way," Seniscal says, "would be the wholesale scattering of silver foil pieces in the areas where they are most likely to be carried down and shaped when the streams and rivers are active; constant monitoring of these areas by radar at the appropriate season would indicate any movement."

Clay frogs: If these frogs were real, reports a Russian scientist, their hearts would communicate via beams of ultraviolet light.

HEART
TO HEART

One disembodied frog heart can control the beating of another at distances up to half an inch, reports a Russian scientist whose article recently appeared in the journal *Psi Research.*

Dr. Gennady Sergeyev began his study by removing two frog hearts and placing each in a separate dish. One heart was left alone, the other given a toxic dose of gitalin, a drug similar to digitalis. The drugged heart slowed and lost its rhythm, as expected. But so did the untouched organ.

When ordinary air or quartz glass separated the two dishes, Sergeyev learned, the hearts stayed synchronized about half the time. But when black paper was used as a barrier, the heartbeats always differed. Thus, Sergeyev has concluded, the organs communicate not through sound but rather by weak beams of ultraviolet light.

This isn't the first time hearts have been controlled at a distance, Sergeyev notes. Recording the electrocardiograms of two persons seated about six feet apart, he says, he discovered that the heartbeat of one mirrored the emotions of the other. And years ago he and Leningrad scientist S. P. Sarychev discovered that prominent psychic Nina Kulagina could stop the beating of an isolated frog heart through mental powers alone.

Is this a dragon or a UFO?

"In every bird, I have a rival."

—*Lucy Audubon*

DRAGON-UFO MIX-UP

Look carefully: The next UFO you see may actually be a flying dragon. The two are easily confused, according to Paul Johnsgard, since "most UFO sightings occur in spring and fall—the seasons for dragon migration." Like UFOs, Johnsgard says, dragons glow in the dark, "probably because they exhale large amounts of methane, which can be ignited by lightning." To produce the dramatic fire-breathing effect, he adds, the European dragon "gnashes its teeth together so violently that sparks fly."

Little-known facts such as these abound in *A Natural History: Dragons and Unicorns,* a book in which University of Nebraska zoologist Johnsgard and his daughter, Karin, apply rigorous scientific methods—mingled with legend and a heavy dose of fantasy—to the study of two mythical creatures. Among their findings: Unicorns evolved from two-horned ancestors; dragons do not devour maidens; and no self-respecting dragon has ever been found with more than one head.

For centuries, the authors note, dragons have been the victims of "bad press" and of self-righteous dragon slayers hoping to "hack their way into history." Unicorns, too, have been abused, especially by men exploiting them for their virgin-detecting abilities. No wonder, says Johnsgard, that "dragon and unicorn populations have continued to decline precipitously in recent years."

Fortunately, the authors promise, these wondrous creatures can still be found "anywhere that the heart and imagination are receptive." In fact they close their book with a field guide.

This woman has become a millionaire with the advice of a psychic.

PSYCHIC STOCK MARKET ANALYSIS

Bevy Jaegers, of Creve Coeur, Missouri, has become a real embarrassment to professional stockbrokers. She predicted five stocks likely to increase in value—and though she based her choice on "psychic premonitions" alone, she outperformed all but one of nineteen stockbrokers.

In a recent test conducted by the *St. Louis Business Journal,* twenty entrants (including Jaegers) submitted the names of five stocks apiece. During the next six months the Dow Jones industrial average—a gauge of stock market performance—fell 8 percent. But Jaegers's stocks went up an average of 17.2 percent (compared with 17.4 percent for the lone stockbroker who bettered her). Sixteen of the stockbrokers finished in the red. If Jaegers had backed her selections with cash—which she didn't—an investment of $5,000 divided equally among the five stocks would have returned $829 profit.

Jaegers says she randomly chooses stocks from Standard and Poor's index of companies, places each company name in an unmarked envelope, and then grasps each envelope separately. "If it's a good stock," she asserts, "the envelope feels hot against my hand."

Jaegers started picking stocks in 1977 and claims to have parlayed an initial investment of $3,000 into $22,000.

For a fifty-dollar annual fee, she'll mail you monthly issues of *Hotline Update,* a newsletter of stock market predictions.

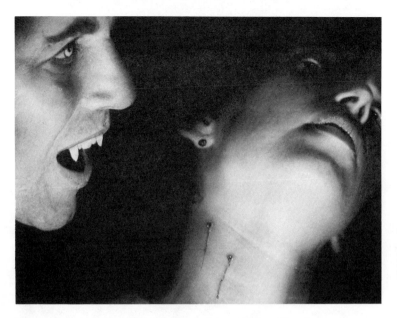

Modern-day vampire: He's driven to violence by an allergic reaction to blood.

DRACULA'S BLOOD

Prince Vlad Tepes, the savage fifteenth-century Transylvanian who became the model for the fictional vampire Dracula, may have been driven mad by an allergic reaction to blood.

That at least is the conclusion of Idaho physician Thomas McDevitt, who says that someone allergic to a substance may also develop an addiction to it. "When deprived of the irritant," he notes, "the allergy victim can react in a bizarre or greatly agitated manner." Thus if Tepes was allergic to blood, he might have become violent when deprived of it.

As evidence for his theory, McDevitt points out that the real-life Tepes reputedly impaled the heads of hundreds of Turks on stakes near his castle, a sign that he "probably did drink blood, both human and animal." Furthermore portraits of Tepes show a man with all the characteristics of an allergy victim —a sallow, pallid complexion, dark circles under the eyes, and even swollen cheeks. Bram Stoker's description of Dracula, with his nostrils flared and teeth bared, McDevitt adds, might simply be a picture of a person trying to breathe through a stuffy nose.

McDevitt admits his view of Tepes, or Dracula, is only a theory, but it bears out his contention that people with allergies can act in strange, cruel, and unpredictable ways.

If Tepes were alive today, McDevitt adds, doctors could probably cure him with modern immunological techniques.

Bulging brain: Inevitable outcome of evolution.

"Starvation in past lives continues to affect the person in the present one, resulting in a compulsion to overeat."

—*Edith Fiore*

COSMIC BRAINS

Humans may be the only intelligent species around today, but the universe should soon be teeming with all sorts of clever creatures. That's the best guess of paleobiologist Dale Russell, of Ottawa's National Museum of Natural Sciences, who says, "Intelligence in the universe may be like a yeast cake—coming up fast."

Russell has been studying the fossil record to determine the increase in earthly brain size—and intelligence—over the millennia. His conclusion: Creatures on Earth seem to be developing larger, better brains at an ever-quickening pace. If the same is true extraterrestrially, Russell reasons, then even if intelligent aliens don't exist now, they could "within a cosmic eye blink."

Scientists who predict the existence of just a *few* intelligent civilizations in the galaxy, Russell says, are being overly conservative. "Their estimates," he explains, "are based on the erroneous assumption that such civilizations will exist for a while, then simply die out. But biology just doesn't work this way."

For instance, he continues, "Though the human species itself may cease to exist, it could give rise to a more clever species. And that group could produce still cleverer descendants. It's also possible," he notes, "for man to be replaced by an entirely different creature; already the parrot, elephant, and dolphin are as large-brained as some of man's ancestors and closest relatives."

Man cannot be as isolated as he seems, Russell maintains. "We haven't yet detected extraterrestrials." But the universe is still evolving, he says, and is most likely full of civilizations just on the brink of technological sophistication, nearly ready to greet us through the vastness of space.

VENUSIAN GARDEN

Venus was long considered the garden planet, a world of rain forests, gigantic tree ferns, mermaids, and towering clouds. But years of research clearly refuted that image, revealing instead a scorching wasteland burdened by enormous pressures, temperatures reaching 900 degrees F., and deadly quantities of carbon dioxide.

Now, however, a French space scientist says he can convert Venus into the Eden we once believed it was. All we need to do, says astronomer Christian Marchal, of the École Polytechnique, in Paris, is shield the planet from the sun until it's cool enough to support life. How? Just place the hostile orb in the shadow of clouds formed by exploding asteroids.

According to Marchal, scientists can get an asteroid near Venus by vaporizing part of its interior with small nuclear bombs. The vaporized rock would then escape as gas, propelling the asteroid forward with a type of nuclear jet engine. Once steered into position between Venus and the sun, the asteroid could be blown apart with larger nuclear bombs. The resulting dust cloud would block the sun and cool Venus down by a few degrees a week, making it temperate enough for human habitation in a decade.

As the planet cooled, he adds, most of the lethal carbon dioxide would drop out of the air, combining with Venusian rocks to form earthlike quartz and calcite. The only task left then would be creating breathable air—easy enough once genetic engineers developed microbes that could secrete oxygen.

Eventually, Marchal concludes, the dust cloud would settle, casting a shadow over the planet's central latitudes. But two lush sunlit regions, each about the size of Europe, would be left at the poles.

> "The KGB is happy
> to promote stories about aliens
> chasing cars and
> boring holes through windows."

UFO
UPDATE

Editor's note: James Oberg, a world-famous meteorologist whose credits in the field would make most experts envious, is surprisingly also an expert on the Soviet space program. He has allowed us a few moments to trace the origin of some very peculiar and enigmatic UFOs.

A giant red crescent surrounded by swirling gas clouds zoomed over central Russia just before midnight on June 14, 1980. Called the most widely witnessed UFO in history, it sent tens of thousands of citizens running through the streets in fear of a nuclear attack. When bombs failed to fall, Russians started whispering about humanoids on the streets of Moscow, weird skin burns, and mysterious holes drilled right through apartment windows.

When news of the UFO finally reached the United States, I read about it in the pages of the *National Enquirer.* I puzzled over the strange object's origin for a while, then recalled tales of an equally bizarre object that had flashed through the skies of Chile, Argentina, Brazil, and Uruguay, also in June 1980. Checking my files, I found that the South American UFO—a fast-moving white halo bigger than the moon—had also made its appearance on June 14, a mere hour after the Soviet sighting.

I'd learned enough about orbital flight from my years at NASA to know that the two sightings, though different in appearance, might be due to a single satellite launched from Earth. But I had to prove it, and I thought I could do just that with data generated by Air Force radars that regularly scan satellite paths worldwide.

I'd soon written to the Goddard Space Flight Center in Greenbelt, Maryland, asking for information about every satellite that had left Earth within a week of the sightings. I'd also sent photos of the Soviet and South American UFOs to computer expert Robert Sheaffer: Sheaffer would analyze the photos to calculate the trajectories of the objects passing through the sky. When both sets of information arrived, I would see whether I could match the UFOs with a particular vehicle.

All the data came by late March 1982, and I shouted, "Eureka!" The reports *were* engendered by a satellite—a Missile Early Warning satellite launched from the supersecret Northern Cosmodrome space center, near the Soviet city of Plesetsk.

The launch was complex, but its unique characteristics could account for the sightings. At liftoff, about 11:55 P.M. Moscow time, twenty engines spewed a crescent of smoke into the skies. As the rocket headed east, the ruddy midnight sun lit the smoke plumes in a dazzling array. An hour later, just as the satellite was passing Argentina, its final stage fired, pushing the payload into space and dumping leftover fuel. That fuel formed a temporary cloud, or halo, illuminated by the evening sun.

I've recently tied two other South American "halos" to Cosmodrome satellites launched on February 11, 1980, and October 31, 1981. Satellites from the Northern Cosmodrome, it seems, can account for UFO sightings around the world. The KGB, eager to muddy the water and cover up public recognition of the military space center at Plesetsk, is only too happy to promote scintillating stories about aliens chasing cars and boring nasty holes through windows.

Hundreds of thousands of Russians saw a fireball streak over the Volga River toward the twilit mountains in the distance. It was a warm May evening in 1967, and the witnesses—everyone from peasants to airplane pilots—watched entranced as the crescent vanished in the eastern sky. But fascination gave way to national hysteria when the fireball kept returning week after week for more than six months. Then, in October of that year, the Soviet Government did something totally out of character: After ignoring the UFO phenomenon for decades, it set up a semiofficial investigative committee, composed of its most gifted astronomers. A few years later, under the auspices of the prestigious Soviet Academy of Sciences, the members issued their analysis: UFOs were *real* and unlike anything known to mankind.

But it was all a sham. The Soviet Government knew the truth behind the UFOs because its own space program was launching them: They were illicit tests of nuclear missiles that orbited the earth, then soared back down over the U.S.S.R. Soviet military officers were no doubt pleased that the world thought of them as space vehicles from another planet, since Moscow had just signed a solemn Outer Space Treaty, forbidding the use of exactly those kinds of orbital weapons. Indeed the Soviet Union managed to deceive people at home and abroad for fifteen years—until I broke the ruse a few months ago.

The cover-up began unraveling when I traced recent UFO sightings in Russia and South America to secret Soviet missile tests. It was clear that the Soviet Government had actually encouraged blatant misinterpretation of its military activities in space.

So when American ufologists began extolling a *new* Soviet report on the 1967 sightings this spring, I smelled a rat. Directed by famed Soviet astronomer Lev Gindilis, the study analyzed reams of new information and concluded once again that UFOs could well be the chariots of alien beings from space.

Contrary to Soviet plan, however, this new report helped me prove the UFOs were caused by Soviet warheads. Using report information never before available in the West, I compared the times and dates of the sightings with Soviet "scientific" satellites registered at the U.N. In 90 percent of the cases the 1967 UFOs had hurtled through the sky just hours after a "scientific" satellite launch. Research satellites would have stayed in orbit for years, of course, but it's obvious that the Russians had been launching *missiles,* which plummet to the ground after a single revolution around Earth.

By trying to prove that UFOs were "real," the Soviet scientists were evidently attempting to show that their illegal space tests were *not* real. Computer scientists have a motto; "Garbage in, garbage out." The Gindilis report used garbage and produced garbage, and the fact that so many Western UFO experts swallowed that garbage so willingly is bound to leave a bad taste in their mouth for years to come.

"We do not hug our
miracles close. We put them
hastily away, preferring
the commonplace to live
with."

—*Fulton Oursler*

These people are wasting their time; new research shows they can reach the dead *without* the formality of a séance.

> "Technology . . . the knack of so arranging the world that we don't have to experience it."
>
> —*Max Frisch*

CONTACTING THE DEAD

Believe it or not, you don't have to go to a spooky séance to speak with those who have passed on. The dead speak with those among the living regularly, in fact, they communicate numerous times during the course of a normal day.

That at least is the startling implication of research recently completed by Julian Burton of the West Side Center for Growth and Counseling in Los Angeles. Burton, who saw a vivid apparition of his mother shortly after she died, discovered the universality of such visions when he conducted a poll on the subject. The psychologist, whose work earned him a doctorate from the International University of Los Angeles, began by distributing questionnaires to psychic-research groups. Of those who returned the questionnaire, a whopping 76 percent reported a postmortem contact at some point in their lives.

Thinking that perhaps his population was biased, Burton distributed another group of questionnaires to students in several psychology departments at Los Angeles County colleges. These results were comparable. In fact no fewer than 55 percent of the students at one rural Christian college reported contacts with the deceased. And older respondents reported such experiences only slightly more commonly than did people eighteen to sixty years of age.

Burton reports that most people glimpsed the visitation in the form of a subjective impression or an especially meaningful dream. Yet close to 20 percent said they saw apparitions, and some 11 percent heard the voices of the dead speaking to them. As might be expected, most of the informants reported that the experience markedly changed their attitudes about the possibility of life after death.

Burton is still not sure what his data meant. Instead of trying to determine whether these contacts are really communiques from the dead, he suggests we ask why so many people are having these experiences and why they so commonly consider them valid.

IN SEARCH OF THE REAL NOAH'S ARK

Colonel James B. Irwin was the daring young astronaut who drove the lunar rover along the surface of the moon in 1971. Today, back on Earth, he is pursuing an equally challenging mission: searching the cliffs of Mount Ararat, Turkey, for the ark allegedly built by Noah.

The *Apollo 15* veteran, founder of the High Flight Foundation, a Christian faith ministry in Colorado Springs, began looking for the ark after meeting Eryl Cummings, of Farmington, New Mexico. Cummings, who has spent forty years seeking biblical artifacts, thought that Irwin's fame would persuade the Turkish Government to permit an expedition. He was right. The Turks even provided a military escort up Ararat, which is just a few miles from the border between the U.S.S.R. and Iran.

"Originally I thought I'd take eight people with me," Irwin says, "since eight traveled in the ark." But he wound up selecting a party of twelve men, with whom he combed the north slope of Ararat three separate times.

Irwin was injured during the first trip in August 1983. Cut off from his group, he was apparently struck on the head by a rock and then fell to the bottom of a canyon where he lay unconscious for about five hours. He came to long enough to crawl into his sleeping bag, and the others found him the next morning. He recovered sufficiently to return that September, though his energy "wasn't up to par" and the third trip, a month later, was cut short by a heavy snowfall.

"The ark thus far has eluded us," Irwin admits, "but next summer, Lord willing, we'll search the northeast side."

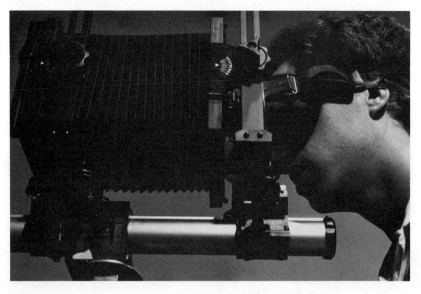

Photographing visions: Can this man capture madness on film?

HALLUCINATION ON FILM

Demons of the mind are what psychotic hallucinations have been called, but now news from the Soviet Union indicates they may be more than that: Psychiatrist G. P. Krokhalev says he has successfully photographed the visions of the insane.

Dr. Krokhalev's techniques are simple. He places skindivers' goggles over the eyes of his actively hallucinating psychotic patients, then covers the goggles with a camera. The patients are instructed to concentrate on their hallucinations while photographs are taken of their eyes.

The resulting prints, Krokhalev says, show shadowy forms that resemble the contents of the hallucinations. Though the forms are not well defined, he contends, a trained eye can recognize them.

Krokhalev's critics charge that these "forms" are only Rorschach-like misinterpretations. But after visiting Krokhalev in his office in Perm, Dr. Stanley Krippner, of the Saybrook Institute in San Francisco, has concluded that while the forms may not be produced by the cornea, they *do* warrant more extensive examination.

Krokhalev says he's meeting this challenge: He's trying to tape-record his patients' auditory hallucinations. He's also eager to find out whether he can project visual hallucinations onto a television screen.

Astrians are perfectly triangular, with two legs at the base and one eye on each side of the upper point.

FLATLAND REDUX

Imagine a hair-thin disk floating in a universe with only two dimensions—length and width. Then picture the rim of that disk swarming with inhabitants, from cats and people to juniper trees.

This sort of two-dimensional fantasy planet was first suggested in 1884 when London clergyman Edwin Abbott Abbott published his satirical novel *Flatland*. Though the book revealed almost nothing about the nature of life on such a world, it *did* pique the imagination of Canadian computer scientist Alexander Dewdney, who several years ago created his own 2-D planet and named it Astria. After hours of intensive thought, Dewdney managed to give the 2-D planet its own laws of physics and chemistry, its own ecology, and even a race of Astrians.

Creating a universe in two dimensions, Dewdney reports, was not easy. Screws, for instance, can't exist without all three dimensions, and neither can wheels with axles. "You can't even design animals with a normal digestive tract," he notes, "because in two dimensions, any opening that passes all the way through the animal cuts it in half."

Given such stringent ground rules, Dewdney remarks, the planet of Astria could only be an infinitely thin pancake of molten rock. A single, flattened continent surrounds most of its rim, and an ocean covers all the rest.

The Astrians themselves are perfectly triangular, with two legs at the base and one eye on each side of the upper point. Without three dimensions they can't walk around one another; therefore, when two of them meet, one must climb over the other to pass by. Their social order centers on the question of who climbs and who is climbed upon.

Though Dewdney did most of the early work on his planet, many others have contributed. English physicist Roger Penrose devised an ingenious set of gears to operate 2-D machinery. Gerontologist Alex Comfort created 2-D beings that could move with ease. Others added a flat steam engine and a chess game using only the king, knight, and rook.

One critic pointed out that Astria's inhabitants had fatal flaws. So Dewdney redesigned them a bit. To mark the change, he also renamed the planet; it is now called Arde.

Dewdney's notes about Arde have now grown enough to fill a book, and his newest work, entitled *The Planiverse,* was published by Poseidon Press in 1984.

"The eye you see is not an
eye because you see it;
it is an eye because it sees
you."

—*Antonio Machado*

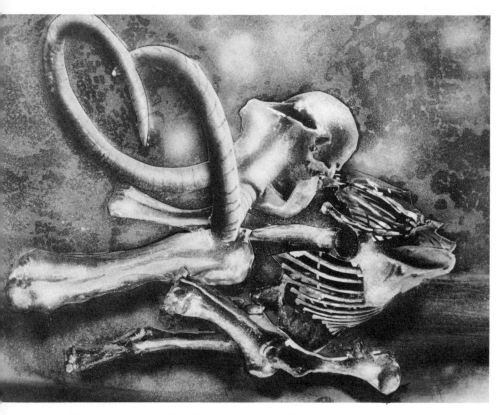

Mammoth skeleton: Was this animal charbroiled
in the Hollywood hills?

LIFE IN
HOLLYWOOD?

The first sign of early *Homo sapiens* was discovered in 1868, when scientists stumbled across the bones of Cro-Magnon man in a rock shelter near Les Eyzies, France. The 35,000-year-old remains were buried alongside chisellike tools and stunning works of art—sure proof of prehistoric civilization. When researchers later found similar specimens nearby, they concluded that intelligent life may have evolved in southern France.

Now Arizona archaeologist Jeffrey Goodman has another theory: He claims that Cro-Magnon-like men and civilization itself evolved in Hollywood, California, or at least a stone's throw away. His evidence? Fossils and tools that indicate the presence of intelligent life in the Los Angeles area as long as 47,000 years ago.

Goodman notes that archaeologists on California's Santa Rosa Island, for instance, recently unearthed a barbecue pit containing charred mammoth skeletons, spearheads, and carving tools. When UCLA radiocarbon-dating expert Rainer Berger analyzed the remains, he found that they were at least 47,000 years old.

Since then, Goodman contends, archaeologists have also begun to "raid" California museums filled with fossils discovered long before radiocarbon dating was ever developed. Researchers scavenging the San Diego Museum have thus far found one 47,000-year-old Cro-Magnon-type skull from Del Mar Beach and another, said to be 45,000 years old, from nearby Oceanside.

To New York City anthropologist Helen Fisher, Goodman's theory is "ridiculous. *Homo sapiens,* like Cro-Magnon man," she says, "probably invaded North America when the Bering Strait—a narrow waterway between Siberia and Alaska—froze to form an ice bridge tens of thousands of years ago."

But Goodman, who expects skeptical scientists to scoff at his theory, says, "America is still number one. Heck, we were the first intelligence on the moon. So why shouldn't we be the first intelligence on Earth too?"

129

TO BUILD
A PYRAMID

Not by myriad slaves nor by divine or UFO intervention were the Egyptian pyramids built, a Boston engineer asserts, but rather with forethought, diligence, and an ingenious contraption known as the wheel.

The secret of assembling the great royal tombs came to John D. Bush soon after he bought an abandoned granite quarry near Gloucester, Massachusetts. Struggling fruitlessly to nudge a sixteen-ton block with wedges and jacks, Bush hit on the idea of making the block the axle of a giant wheel. He built four pieces of curved wood and strapped each one to a different corner of the block. He was then able to roll the boulder with relative ease. The technique worked so well, he felt somebody must have thought of it before.

The engineering problems of building the pyramids seemed the most obvious parallel, Bush says. So he looked up texts about ancient Egyptian masonry and found a device called a "cradle" that was a dead ringer for his makeshift contraption. But the archaeologist-authors guessed that the cradle had been used as a wedge. "It never occurred to them that you need a set of *four* cradles to get anywhere," Bush asserts. "But then they were sitting down with an artifact, trying to figure out its use. I was trying to move stone."

At an outdoor demonstration Bush staged recently in Boston, crews of six to ten out of shape volunteers found they could haul 2.5-ton concrete blocks up a steep ramp almost effortlessly on the cradle principle. With the help of a similar device, Bush concludes, a few thousand Egyptian laborers could have built a pyramid in twenty years.

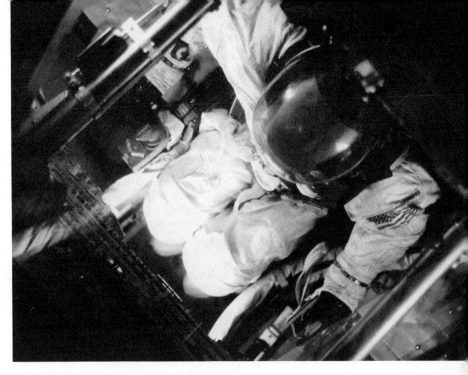

Future terrorist: This man will be punished
in the vastness of space.

SERVING TIME
IN SPACE

The first wave of settlers in space is bound to consist of explorers, adventurers, and scientists. Liken this to the early Spanish explorers who first came to the New World in the fifteenth and sixteenth centuries. But the second wave could well consist of murderers, rapists, and terrorists, a Canadian criminologist contends.

Overcrowding in prisons is worsening as prospects for space colonies improve, observes Essat Fattah of Simon Fraser University in British Columbia, and these trends support the establishment of extraterrestrial jails.

"This is not something I'd like to see happen," Fattah says. "It is a prediction based on a historical reading of social control." In the eighteenth century, Fattah reports, the British solved the problems of crowded, expensive-to-maintain prisons and the need for cheap labor in the new colonies by transporting criminals to America and Australia. In the twenty-first century, history will repeat itself, especially since the likely abolition of capital punishment will lead to an ever-increasing prison population in facilities already at maximum capacity.

Fattah explores this thesis fully in his forthcoming book *Are Prisons Necessary?* in which he also discusses other technological alternatives to incarceration. "It will be possible in the near future to control movement without immobilization," Fattah says, "to curb violence without segregation, and to protect society without incarceration." For example, surgically implanted radio devices could be used to monitor the location of a prisoner; if the prisoner stepped beyond a certain geographic limit, guards could quickly track him down and return him to justice.

Fattah predicts that only the fiercest criminals will inhabit jails in space; after all, it would be most economical to send only those convicts with life sentences.

"And there's a dreadful law here—
it was made by mistake,
but there it is—that if anyone
asks for machinery, they have
to have it and keep on using it."

—*E. Nesbit*

NEAR-DEATH
PREDICTIONS

Those about to die often see their lives flash before them. But according to psychologist Kenneth Ring of the University of Connecticut, people who recover from bouts of clinical death report glimpses of the future as well.

To study the visions of near-death prophets, Ring traveled the country, tape-recording talks with more than a dozen survivors. One of his subjects, for instance, was a man who had nearly succumbed to appendicitis in 1941 at the age of ten. During the operation, he told Ring, he saw himself grown up and married with two children. He envisioned himself sitting in an armchair, aware of something "very strange" behind the wall.

This very scene suddenly unfolded one day in 1968, the man told Ring, "when I sat in a chair, reading a book, and happened to glance at my children. I realized that *this* was the memory from 1941. And the strange object behind the wall was a forced-air heater, something not in my sphere of knowledge as a child."

Ring heard subject after subject report uncanny premonitions of things that they say have since come true. But he was most impressed by those who related visions about the fate of the world.

Indeed, almost all of Ring's subjects have prophesied a disastrous epoch that they assert will begin in a decade or less. Some have foreseen earthquakes, volcanoes, and droughts; others, famine and nuclear war. While most of us undoubtedly would perish in the decades of destruction, Ring's subjects say that peace will ultimately prevail. "The trouble will be transitory rather than total," they contend, with decades of worldwide brotherhood to follow.

Ring, however, doesn't really take these visions literally. "I'm inclined to think the prophecies are metaphors for the fears and hopes of the subconscious," he says. "As the near-death victim is jolted to awareness, he might perceive a symbolic earthquake or volcanic eruption. As he calms down and enters a period of serenity, he might sense universal brotherly love."

Attorney Peter Gersten: As a boy he read every flying-saucer magazine he could get his hands on.

"Classified UFO
documents lay in the
dungeons and
bins of every spy agency."

UFO
UPDATE

By day, attorney Peter Gersten fights drug and murder raps for a host of Bronx defendants. But at night, from a modest storefront office in the shadows of the Bronx County Courthouse, he works on another sort of case: proving UFOs are technically advanced vehicles threatening our very existence.

Gersten developed his passion for UFOs as a boy, when he read every flying-saucer magazine he could get his hands on. Years later, as a lawyer, he subscribed to a UFO clipping service. When articles on UFO sightings from around the world poured in, he began to suspect that his childhood beliefs had some validity; so he wrote to numerous UFO organizations, volunteering his help.

Then, in September 1977, he received a surprise visit from W. Todd Zechel, research director for an Arizona-based group called Ground Saucer Watch. Zechel wanted some classified Central Intelligence Agency documents describing a 1952 UFO film made by an ex-marine; he thought a lawsuit could win him the right to see them. Gersten quickly agreed to represent Ground Saucer Watch, but he widened the lawsuit to include *any* UFO document in the CIA's possession. Using the Freedom of Information Act, he pried some nine hundred documents from dusty CIA bins in less than a year.

Reports on the 1952 film, Gersten explains, revealed nothing new. But information in some of the other documents seemed frightening. In October, November, and December 1975, for instance, military personnel across the northern United States had reported unexplained objects hovering over nuclear-missile and bomber bases. One government analysis even suggested Americans deal with UFOs by developing a series of adequate defense measures "in a minimum amount of time."

Gersten soon learned that classified UFO documents lay in the dungeons of most spy agencies, including the Defense Intelligence Agency, the National Security Agency, and the Federal Bureau of Investigation. Again wielding the Freedom of Information Act, he procured two thousand additional reports: In one he discovered that UFOs over Kuwait had allegedly damaged the pumping system of the Kuwait Oil Company. Another document stated that Iranian pilots had lost control of their jets during an encounter with "inordinately maneuverable" UFOs. And still another told of "strange machines" near military bases in Algeria.

By 1980 Gersten had formed a group called Citizens Against UFO Secrecy. Its purpose: to obtain 233 documents still locked in government coffers. These efforts have recently been stymied, however, since the courts decided that releasing more documents would expose American intelligence-gathering techniques.

Nevertheless Gersten contends that he still has "enough information to prove that UFOs pose a threat." The government doesn't agree. But Gersten says, "We'll just let the people decide."

> "I'm a strong believer in reincarnation. To me it's as real as getting up in the morning, strolling along the boulevard on a warm day, taking a gondola in Venice, walking along the Champs Élysées, or attending the Mardi Gras in New Orleans."
>
> —*Kenny Kingston*

TRAVEL BY PROXY

It's a rainy Sunday. You call the foreign city of your choice and order a proxy: a small robot equipped with TV cameras, audio intercoms, artificial arms, and wheels. Then, with your home TV hooked to the robot by satellite, you're set for a day along the *Champs Élysées* or Oxford Street—without ever leaving your living room.

Just flick on your TV set, says David Yates, the London computer scientist who thought up this scheme, and city streets instantly appear on the screen. Since your set is equipped with a steering wheel, you might begin driving your proxy toward the city's marketplace. Once there you could instruct it to pick out souvenirs, bargain with shop owners, and have the purchases sent to your home.

While early-model proxies might provide only visual and auditory information, Yates speculates, later models would give their owners a complete sensory experience. You'll actually taste that frothy cappucino from the café in Rome and feel that luxurious Japanese silk. "Scientists have already electronically linked an amputee's nervous system to an artificial limb, making it possible for him to feel what his limb feels," Yates explains, "so perhaps a technological advance will make a similar link between a traveler and a proxy—without amputation."

But don't throw out that Club Med membership, at least not yet. The high cost of a proxy's sophisticated equipment, Yates admits, will make it unaffordable to the average consumer for years. And even when the price comes down, critics will have to be appeased. After all, as they legitimately note, criminals might steal the proxies and use them to mug the elderly, rob banks, or murder.

Victim of inexperience: Funeral directors sometimes ask untrained wives and daughters to style hair for the deceased.

HAIRDRESSING FOR THE DEAD

Noella Popagno of Hollywood, Florida, has written the world's first and only textbook on desairology—the art of hairdressing for the deceased.

"In the past," Popagno explains, "funeral directors gave the task of hair-styling to their untrained wives or daughters. So accidents would happen. One woman, for instance, ironed a corpse's hair until it turned yellow and fell out. Now imagine how the family felt at the wake when they approached the casket."

To avoid such disasters, Popagno tries to get professional beauticians involved by dispelling their overriding fear: that the dead will move about. The deceased, Popagno admits, do flinch or twitch from time to time, whenever embalming fluids make their muscles contract. "But," she adds, "in thirty-five years of working with the dead, I've never seen anybody sit up and crack a joke."

Popagno's manual is designed to prepare hairdressers for those situations that never pop up with live subjects. Take the case of a customer who's had a cranial autopsy. In that instance the subject has a horseshoe incision cut along the crest of the scalp and from ear to ear. Since the scalp may be sewn back so that hairs mix with the thread, Popagno warns, "it's advisable to hold tresses in place while combing, rolling, and styling. Otherwise you might see the entire scalp fall off.

"Families need an acceptable last image of the deceased to help them get over the shock of the death," Popagno says. "And the desairologist is a crucial part of that process." Anyone interested in entering the field, she adds, can purchase a copy of *Desairology* from J. J. Publishing, 1312 Arthur Street, Hollywood, FL 33109.

> "He tried to
> contact it with radio messages
> in Portuguese and
> English. Then he tried telepathy."

UFO UPDATE

The overnight flight from the Brazilian metropolis of Fortaleza south to São Paulo started off routinely enough. Passengers settled into their seats on the VASP airliner, and as rows of interior lights dimmed, most people dozed off. But the predawn quiet was broken by the crackling voice of the pilot, Gerson Maciel De Britto. "I see a strange object forty or fifty miles to the left," he announced. "And I need eyewitnesses."

Now wide awake, passengers found themselves bathed in a blinding light; they scrambled to the windows and for the next hour and twenty-two minutes watched the sky flash red, orange, white, and blue.

Observing from the cockpit, De Britto said he saw what seemed like "a fast-moving, saucer-shaped disk with five spotlights." He tried to contact it by sending radio messages in Portuguese and English. When that failed, he concentrated hard, hoping to send or receive telepathic messages "mind to mind."

Just before landing in Rio de Janeiro for a scheduled stopover, De Britto reported the light was a mere eight miles from the plane and closing in fast. The radar picked up absolutely nothing, but when the Rio tower asked three commercial pilots flying in the area whether they saw the dazzling light, the answer was affirmative. Soon a group of Brazilian military planes had joined the hunt. Although this group publicly claimed it found nothing, the official report remains classified.

In all, nearly one hundred people saw the brilliant object. And that morning, February 8, 1982, every major Brazilian newspaper carried a front-page account of the story. In the days following, reporters from newspapers, television stations, and national magazines such as *Veja* and *Manchete* tracked down UFO experts for an explanation. They soon learned that on February 8, Venus had risen in the eastern sky at 3:10 A.M.

Could Venus give off such an intense and colorful light? Yes, says Dr. J. Allen Hynek, director of the Center for UFO Studies in Evanston, Illinois.

"Venus has a thick atmosphere that acts like a prism. When it's rising and low in the sky, it can twinkle in different colors. When it's high, it could appear to give off a glow."

All well and good, but De Britto claimed he saw Venus in addition to the eerie light. Moreover, he said, the light seemed intelligent, maintaining the same orientation to the plane even after he changed course by fifty-one degrees. Hynek says, "If what the pilot says is true, then it could not have been Venus. If it wasn't Venus, then it was a UFO."

A week after the sighting, it was carnival time in Brazil, and talk of the blazing UFO began to fade. "Such things are less disturbing to the mystical sensibility of Brazilians than they would be to more incredulous Americans," explains Roberto Muggiatti, one of *Manchete*'s editors.

That sensibility is best illustrated by passenger Elaine Belashi, a philosophy teacher. "What it was I really don't know," she reflects. "Just as we have our planes, they must have theirs."

"You are a fluke of the
Universe./You have no right
to be here."

—*"Deteriorata"*

Hypnotism: Does it elicit true past-life memories or fanciful fabrications?

REMEMBERING PAST LIVES

When regressed back to childhood and beyond, hypnotic subjects often "recall" previous lives in distant eras and cultures. Sometimes the subjects even come up with uncannily accurate historical information. But according to *All in the Mind,* a new book by British author Ian Wilson, many of the most highly touted reincarnation claims can be explained by hidden memories based on the subject's present-life reading and experience.

Wilson did his research by attending regression sessions and listening to numerous tape recordings allegedly describing prior existences. Then, ferreting out historical factors, he read dozens of books and traveled thousands of miles to check the evidence. In case after case he found that subjects had drawn their detailed stories from readily available sources.

One woman that Wilson studied, for instance, remembered being tried for witchcraft in sixteenth-century Chelmsford, England. Her story and the historical information were impressive enough. But she said her trial took place in 1556, although the real Chelmsford trials were held in 1566. A seemingly trivial error, perhaps, but Wilson subsequently learned that the chronicle upon which most contemporary authors base their information dated the Chelmsford trials in 1556 as well.

In another instance, Wilson studied an Englishwoman who had recalled an entire series of past lives under hypnosis, including one in the Roman Britain of the fourth century A.D. Wilson traced much of her information, including fictitious names, to a historical novel by Louis de Wohl.

Though there are some people who may be disappointed to see reincarnation undermined, Wilson believes that his findings are all for the good. They prove that we all hold within ourselves "a dynamic, ever-restless kaleidoscope of images," he says, "the complexity of which we have scarcely begun to grasp."

This young man is typing a message from beyond.

I became interested in
syphilis when I worked for a
time at a mental hospital full
of GPI cases. I discovered
there was a correlation between
the spirochete and mad talent.

—*Anthony Burgess*

WALK-INS

Every morning author Ruth Montgomery places her fingers over the typewriter keys and meditates. Then presto: Words tumble onto the page, dictated straight from the mouths of spirits. In fact Montgomery says that's how she's written all her books, including her bestseller about psychic Jeane Dixon.

One day recently the spirits startled Montgomery with a prediction: In the year 2000 Earth will shift off its axis, unleashing quakes and tidal waves. But the human race will persevere, thanks to walk-ins—spiritual saviors who take over the bodies of lackluster people on the brink of physical or emotional collapse.

Communicating by means of the typewriter, Montgomery's supernatural informants have revealed the names of numerous people possessed by walk-in spirits throughout history, including Jesus Christ, Christopher Columbus, and Charles Colson.

The lives of seventeen living walk-ins have become the subject of Montgomery's new book, *Threshold to Tomorrow*. She writes, for instance, about Swedish scientist Björn Ortenheim, who was sitting on a windswept beach plotting suicide when the brilliant soul of Albert Einstein entered his body. Today, Montgomery says, Ortenheim is refining Einstein's theory of relativity. (He's already changed $E = mc^2$ to $E = mc^4$.)

Another walk-in is the late Egyptian president Anwar Sadat. During World War II Sadat was an angry, dispirited revolutionary languishing in a prison cell. Then, Montgomery contends, "a great Egyptian soul" walked into his body, creating the powerful head of state. Sadat's soul, she adds, may very well return to help solve the Mideast crisis—this time with a new name and appearance.

Montgomery's claims may seem spurious to some. But at least her publisher, G. P. Putnam's Sons in New York, is convinced. *Threshold to Tomorrow*, the company declares, is a "survival manual to the new age."

143

REFUGEES
IN SPACE

Suppose you were faced with fifty million refugees. Where would you put them?

Tackling this problem toward the end of World War II, the United States Government formed a plan to ship refugees into outer space—at least according to the controversial February-March 1983 issue of *Mother Jones* magazine. The plan, says *Mother Jones,* was developed as part of "M" Project, a classified report on world migration commissioned by President Franklin D. Roosevelt in 1942.

Philadelphia librarian Sandy Meredith found a summary of "M" Project in Temple University archives and took it to writer Bob Sanders, who collaborated with her on the *Mother Jones* article. What struck them as most callous and monstrous, they said, was a "chapter . . . titled 'Interstellar Migration,' " in which "M" Project director Henry Field suggested that "temporary quarters" for the homeless might be built "on Venus or Mars."

Some investigation, though, shows that the *Mother Jones* story went a touch too far. Meredith admits, for instance, that "Interstellar Migration" was incorrectly called a chapter when it was merely a subsection of a subsection. She and Sanders also neglected to mention that in the very first line of "Interstellar Migration," Field called his discussion just a "highly impracticable . . . flight of fancy." The reason for the journalists' tactics? "We wanted the story to be read," says Meredith, "not moldering on a back shelf in some obscure little left-wing magazine."

Even with the facts straight, however, the thrust of "M" Project gives one pause. Field not only admits that Roosevelt planned "some forced migration"; he also gives evidence in the summary that as far as he was concerned extraterrestrial immigration might have been more than a passing whim. Describing an attempt he once made to establish contact with outer space by longwave radio, Field concludes, "We shall know the answer" about life on other planets "within forty years."

EEEEEE'S DROPPING

When Judy Reeves returned from a hard day at the office a few years back, she found her Belleville, Illinois, home surrounded by one hundred pieces of metal, each one five inches long and shaped like a capital *E*.

Collecting the letters from her pavement, her garage, and even her tomato patch, she began to fear that the sharp metal prongs could hurt her eight-year-old daughter Kim and other neighborhood children. To prevent another attack, she vowed to trace the *E*'s to their source.

"At first I thought kids had flung them at my house," Reeves says. "But later I found some *E*'s embedded an inch deep in my roof—much too deep for child's play. I realized they must have fallen from the sky."

Reeves then assumed that the *E*'s had been dropped from an airplane as part of a military exercise at nearby Scott Air Force Base. But federal aviation inspector Troy Simms soon convinced her that if the letters had fallen from a plane, they'd have scattered like leaves, covering the entire neighborhood.

She was still baffled when she received a call from Illinois Power Company engineers, who had heard of the *E*'s in the local news. The letters, they said, seemed identical in size and shape to the tin-alloy guts of their electrical transformers. After studying the letters, however, Illinois Power denied all responsibility. "It would have taken a spectacular explosion and an incredible power failure to send this metal hurling onto someone's roof," says company spokesman James Shipp. "But we've had none of that. Maybe they fell from a manufacturer's delivery truck. But if so, then don't ask how they got into the sky."

To Reeves, who thinks that Illinois Power may be trying to avoid a lawsuit, the *E*'s remain a mystery. She lives in dread of the day another metal shower destroys her garden or strikes her on the head. "But," she adds, "my neighbors' jokes are the worst of it. I don't go a day without someone saying, 'Heard your house was bugged; you know, *EEEEEE*'s dropping.'"

"In the morning when we
rise from bed, although
surprised to find ourselves
still alive, we are even more
amazed to find everything
just as we left it the night
before."

—Tommaso Landolfi

COLLEGE FOR
WITCH DOCTORS

Time was, in Zimbabwe, when young healers studied medicinal herbs and roots in the bush, under the guidance of an elder witch-doctor mentor. But now many budding witch doctors attend Zimbabwe Herbal College, earn their TMP (Traditional Medical Practitioner) degree, and then intern at a healing clinic.

When ready to open a practice, the graduate plunks down twenty dollars and joins the 15,000-member Zimbabwe Traditional Healers Association, the witch doctor's AMA.

"Eighty percent of the patients in Zimbabwe turn to witch doctors," claims the president and founder of the healers association, Gordon Chavunduka, TMP. "Many of our members use incantations or speak to the spirits; they wear beads and feathers." But despite such superstitious practice, they still refer patients to M.D.'s for the treatment of certain maladies.

Chavunduka, also chairman of the sociology department at the University of Zimbabwe, makes radio and TV appearances to promote a positive image for witch doctors. "The practitioner does not collect a fee," he notes, "until a patient recovers."

Herbs and roots, when ground into powder or boiled in tea, reportedly cure backaches, mental illness, cancer, and, for an extra fee of twenty dollars, infertility.

KUDZU JESUS

Hundreds of people traveled to the tiny mining town of Holden, West Virginia, to stare at a popular tree covered with kudzu vines. The reason for the pilgrimage? The profile of Jesus Christ, people claimed, seemed to shine from the tree's thick foliage.

The tangled kudzu vines, leaves, and branches didn't seem particularly strange in broad daylight. But late at night, with streetlights aglow, the tree appeared to take on the solemn image of a praying Jesus as portrayed in religious paintings.

The thirty-foot-tall tree's unusual shape was first discovered in September 1982, when a group of men had a few too many drinks in a nearby deserted building, explains Brenda Bingess, a Holden resident. Word quickly spread, and visitors from throughout West Virginia and neighboring states soon created traffic jams as they flocked to see the kudzu Christ.

While some visitors called the tree "spooky," others labeled it "a miracle" and "a sign of things to come." But no matter what their opinion, says resident Joan Means, "they were reverent, like they were in church."

Regardless of its meaning, though, the kudzu Jesus of Logan County is now a thing of the past. Cold weather killed the vines, and the tree itself is doomed: A highway will soon be built right over the spot.

REAL RAIDER OF
THE LOST ARK

His name is Jones. He's fought Arabs and eluded unscrupulous competitors, escaped from deadly vipers and crashing boulders. He's even searching for the Ark of the Covenant.

But he's not the movie character Indiana Jones of *Raiders of the Lost Ark*. He's Vendyl Jones, head of the Institute for Judaic-Christian Studies, based in Israel and Texas.

The similarities between Indiana and Vendyl are more than coincidental. Phil Kaufman, who wrote the story on which the movie is based, worked with Jones on an archaeological dig near Jerusalem in 1977. "Phil asked me if he could do a story based in part on things that happened to me," related Jones. "He took some events and romanticized them."

It could be argued that some of Jones's adventures have been even more difficult and dramatic than the Hollywood version. For example, the real-life Jones escaped from a site booby-trapped with not one but four gigantic bouncing boulders. (A member of the excavation party jumped off a cliff to avoid being crushed.)

And though Indiana Jones *found* the Lost Ark, Vendyl is still searching. Before he determines the whereabouts of the Ark, however, he'd like to locate the ashes of the Red Heifer, an ancient cow that was allegedly sacrificed and burned. Once the Red Heifer has been found, legend has it, the mystical power of the Ark will be restored.

Working with his own translation of the Copper Scroll (one of the Dead Sea Scrolls), Jones has already found some twenty reference points allegedly leading to the Heifer—including a plaster floor, two man-made niches in the wall of a cave, and a burial rock with white sand beneath it. If his interpretation is correct, then the Heifer's ashes will be found in a bronze vessel, with the Ark buried somewhere nearby.

Finding the Heifer and then the Ark, says Jones, will have enormous religious significance. "According to Judaism," he points out, "the Sanhedrin Court (the highest Jewish council) will be reestablished, temple worship will be reinstated, and Jews from all over the world will return to Israel."

> "The nausea, the
> blisters, the low blood count—
> it's just like the
> survivors of Hiroshima and Nagasaki."

UFO
UPDATE

Three Texans, the federal government, and a colossal diamond-shaped flying machine are about to come head to head in one of the most disturbing UFO cases in history.

The story began on the chilly winter evening of December 29, 1980, when Betty Cash, Vickie Landrum, and Vickie's grandson, Colby Landrum, were driving through the woods to their home in Dayton, Texas. Traveling through an especially deserted stretch, they looked up ahead to see a hovering diamond-shaped object spitting a jet of searing flame. Afraid they were about to be killed, the trio briefly got out of the car to escape the heat. After the craft flew off, they continued down the road. Rounding a turn, they saw the craft again, this time followed by more than twenty helicopters.

In the following months Betty and Vickie, both only in their fifties, lost much of their hair; when it later grew back, it was thinner, drier, and grayer. Holes developed in Vickie's fingernails. She developed a cataract in her right eye, and the vision in her left narrowed until she was looking through a small cone of light. Seven-year-old Colby, whose vision had been perfect, began wearing glasses. All three suffered from nausea and weakness.

The following year the situation got worse. Betty had a heart attack as well as a stroke that temporarily paralyzed her. Vickie and Colby broke out in sores that permanently scarred their face and limbs. Colby has had anemia, and doctors say he might develop leukemia.

"There's no doubt," says the radiologist on the case, "that they were exposed to a broad spectrum of radiation. The nausea, the hair falling out, the blisters, the low blood count—it's just like the survivors of Hiroshima and Nagasaki." It would certainly help treatment, he adds, "if we could find out exactly what type was involved."

That information is not available, however, since the government has denied any knowledge of the craft. Investigations led by McDonnell Douglas engineer John Schuessler have turned up a number of witnesses to the helicopters, repeatedly identified as a military-type Chinook aircraft. But even the

Army Inspector General could produce no admissions from any branch of the military.

The treatment has also been limited because the victims have run out of money. Neither Vickie nor Betty can work. Totally incapacitated, Betty has gone to Alabama to live with her mother. Vickie can't see well enough to drive or do desk work, and her sores and scars are too unsightly to allow her to work with the public. So even though she needs a new prescription for her glasses and though Colby has developed knots the size of thumbs in his knee joints, neither has been to a doctor in several months.

Now, down to perhaps their last hope, they are taking their case before the courts, seeking damages from the government, along with access to hidden information that might help them. "I love my country," Vickie says, "but the country's supposed to make you free, and in my heart I know it's chained me to misery."

"For whatever a man may
do, he does it in order to
annihilate time, in order to
revoke it, and that revocation
is called space."

—*Hermann Broch*

UFO DETECTORS

According to some avid flying-saucer watchers, the well-equipped home should have not only smoke detectors and a burglar-alarm system but also a UFO detector. Although do-it-yourself plans can be purchased at a reasonable price, most buyers prefer the ready-made models.

Shields Enterprises, in Emmaus, Pennsylvania, for example, sells more than three hundred detectors annually. Designed to detect the strong electromagnetic fields often associated with UFOs, the Shields device consists of a magnetic reed switcher, a buzzer, and a battery, in a metal container. To activate it, users place the box on a window ledge inside the home and position an accompanying detector probe outside the window. When electromagnetic energy is high, the alarm sounds. In addition, the battery and detector can be tested by depressing a red button on the front panel.

Some ufologists protest that since not all UFOs demonstrate electromagnetic properties, overconfident detector owners might waste their nights in slumber while fleets of extraterrestrial spaceships pass over their rooftops. Critics also claim that most magnetic detectors fall into two categories: those that remain obstinately silent because they are unresponsive to any but the strongest magnetic fields, and those that are oversensitive, sending hopeful UFO observers rushing to their windows at all hours of the day and night.

Despite the controversy, consumers continue to buy the devices. Its manufacturer has never received a request for a refund.

> "Belief is not the beginning
> but the end of all
> knowledge."
>
> —*Johann Wolfgang*
> *von Goethe*

POE TOASTER

Every January 19 since 1949, someone has crept into Baltimore's Westminster Churchyard, placing roses and cognac on the 134-year-old grave of Edgar Allan Poe. The occasion: the great poet's birthday. But in 1983 Jeff Jerome, the curator of Poe House, decided to find out who the mysterious gift bearer was.

To stake out the writer's grave, Jerome and four other Poe buffs secluded themselves in the Westminster catacombs. Then, to pass the hours, they tried to interpret (for the umpteenth time) the eerie ritual of the "Poe Toaster"—the nickname they'd given to the person who yearly toasted Poe. Why, for instance, did the phantom always leave three roses? Was it because Poe had used the word "rose" many times in his books?

The questions poured out until 1:30 A.M., when the small troupe heard a stir. A flashlight crept across the crypts, and someone rattled the cemetery gates as the group rushed through Westminster to confront the toaster. But only Jerome and twenty-one-year-old student Ann Byerly caught a glimpse of the culprit as he sped away.

"I saw the top of his head; he had blond or brown hair," says Byerly. "Then, all of a sudden, he darted from the grave and leaped over a cemetery wall. He was wearing a frock coat, and it was flying open as he ran. It was very dramatic."

"The man," Jerome adds, "was clutching a walking stick with a golden sphere on its end—like the one Poe carried. And before vanishing over the wall, he raised his cane high in the air and shook it at us triumphantly."

Since the stakeout, Jerome has received hundreds of letters from Baltimore residents. A note from one angry man sums up the reaction: "Hey, this stinks. We don't want to know anymore. This is a nice little mystery, and there aren't a lot of mysteries left."

From now on, Jerome promises, he'll let the toaster be.

Stuffed bear: Can this
creature rise from the dead?

ANIMAL
RESURRECTION

Folks in the quiet Dutch village of Eerbeek were going about their workaday lives when they caught the stench of rotting meat. The source of the smell: the backyard of taxidermist John Roeleveld, seventy-two. Spurred by the unbearable odor, Police Sergeant John Hartgers decided to dig into the case. To his utter amazement, he unearthed 250,000 animals that had been stuffed and preserved.

When questioned about the collection—including camels, kangaroos, cats, birds, crocodiles, apes, dogs, and even elephant skulls—Roeleveld was quick to explain. God had instructed him to collect two animals of every species before floodwaters arrived in June 1983. The waters would wipe out evil sinners and copulators, Roeleveld believed, leaving only him, his wife, and the animals to repopulate the world.

Hartgers points out that Roeleveld didn't trap, kill, and stuff all the animals himself. He bought specimens like the hundred-year-old stuffed bear from antique shops. And he used his professional credentials to procure beasts that had died in zoos.

Nevertheless the people of Eerbeek decided that Roeleveld could not go unpunished. Since he was too old for jail, they gave him a $500 fine. They also confiscated his collection in hopes of using it to start a new museum.

"We know no more our own
destiny than a tea leaf
knows the destiny of the
East India Company."

—*Douglas Adams*

MOONDAY

Young Christian Marchal was gazing at the dazzling night sky some thirty years ago, when he had a brainstorm: By placing mirrors on the moon, he could reflect enough light back to Earth to turn night into day. Now a scientist at France's National Office of Aerospace Study and Research, Marchal says he's making that vision a reality.

To create the lunar mirrors, Marchal is currently coating Kapton (a plastic used in spacesuits) with an ultrathin metal surface. Right now his work is experimental, but once the ideal mirror has been built, he predicts, it will be mass-produced and shipped to the moon by shuttle. On the moon, he adds, robots will arrange the mirrors to reflect the light of the sun.

Light reflected back to Earth, Marchal explains, will depend on the area covered by mirrors. About 772 square miles of mirrors, for instance, would provide the light of streetlamps. And with 77,220 square miles of mirrors, Marchal's ultimate goal, the moon would glow like a giant bulb, providing the entire planet with the light of a sunrise or sunset. (During the new moon, of course, we would receive no light at all.)

According to Marchal, his so-called moonday will enable people in tropical climates to work at night, slashing energy costs worldwide. And, he says, there will be few ecological repercussions, with 77,220 square miles of mirrors increasing Earth's temperature by a mere 5 percent.

What about all those night owls who thrive on dark, romantic, candlelit evenings? "They'll adapt," Marchal says. "Men never have trouble adjusting to better conditions."

MYSTERY MISSILE

The Second World War ended more than thirty years ago. So how did a missile from that era end up crashing into the backyard of a suburban house in Lakewood, California, recently? That's a question the Federal Aviation Administration (FAA) and the Los Angeles County sheriff's department would like answered.

The twenty-two-pound shell whistled through a sunny afternoon sky and then plummeted onto the patio of Fred Simons's home—smashing a layer of concrete before coming to rest in a four-foot-deep crater. After digging up the missile, the local bomb squad declared it a dud that contained no explosives.

Because Lakewood is in the flight path of aircraft using the Long Beach Airport, FAA investigators at first theorized that a prankster had probably dropped the shell out of a passing plane.

"We monitored all tapes from around the time the missile hit to see if any aircraft flying over could have opened a door and thrown something out. We would have heard a screaming sound on the tape if that had happened," explains Ben Harris of the FAA. "But we didn't come up with anything."

The Los Angeles County sheriff's department launched a probe to look into other possible explanations. "We never found any source," Deputy Wes Slider comments, "although we determined that the shell could not have been fired from some kind of tube or a cannon."

Lacking any clues at all, both the FAA and the sheriff's department have dropped their investigations of the mystery missile. Harris concludes: "We just have no idea where the thing came from. To tell you the truth, I don't think we'll ever know what happened."

Tin-can coat: This woman thinks it will protect her
from government mind control.

ZAPPED

Dorothy Burdick, a hospital dietician and mother of three, was making love to her husband when she had an unusual thought: "Dorothy, you're being programmed." Then, to her husband's dismay, she burst into tears.

Burdick (a pseudonym she uses so friends won't think she's crazy) took her husband's advice and saw a psychiatrist. But when he was unable to stop the thoughts, she turned to her brother—a kind of Phantom of the Opera whose name can't be revealed, Burdick claims, because "he's working on the H-bomb at MIT." Still, he's the one who supposedly gave her the inside scoop: The United States Government is using Burdick as part of a top-secret experiment in "zapping," or long-distance mind control.

"Some people might think that's nuts," says Burdick. "But they've forgotten our government's long history of experimentation on citizens." In 1956 for instance the U.S. Army admitted to secretly spraying an unknown substance in New York City subway tunnels. And more recently in December 1980, a member of the Canadian Parliament claimed that a CIA-financed psychiatrist tried to brainwash her.

The zapping technique used on Burdick, though, is even more sophisticated: A laser telescope at a nearby Air Force station, the Cape Cod dietician declares in her recent book *Such Things Are Known,* is scanning her house and analyzing the electrical impulses in her brain with a computer.

"In fact," she says, "I'm sure that the computer can decode my brain impulses just as telegraphers decode Morse code. For example, *dot/dot/dot* . . . *dash/dash/dash* . . . *dot/dot/dot* in Morse code means 'SOS', or 'help.' Likewise scientists have found that *dot, dot* in my head means 'Dorothy.' Now that they know the code, they're shooting dots into my head and programming my thoughts. I mean, why else would I wake up every morning to a chorus of voices chanting obscenities? There's just one logical answer: They're zapping me!"

To fend off the ominous laser, Burdick now wears a coat with tin cans tied around it. She also wears a peaked hat filled with marbles.

EXOTIC WEAPONS ACCESS BOOK

Do you want a pocket flamethrower? Have a yen for nonmetallic knives you can sneak through airport security? Or are you just tired of winding your own strangling wire and looking for somewhere to buy it ready-made?

If you've answered yes, we have just what you need: *Exotic Weapons: An Access Book* by Michael Hoy. Published by Loompanics Unlimited of Port Townsend, Washington, the volume answers the age-old question "How can I get across Central Park at night?"

Loompanics specializes in survivalist and terrorist literature—police manuals, lock-picking tutorials, even books telling how to drive getaway cars and build basement nukes. With its list of more than five hundred dealers in the tools of mayhem, *Exotic Weapons* fits their line.

Most weapons, no matter how arcane, can be obtained from a variety of sources. Some seventeen distributors offer the *marikiqusari* and other Oriental equivalents of a bicycle chain. Two supply *calthrops,* tire-shredding spikes to be scattered in front of pursuing vehicles. Four deal in sword canes. No fewer than twenty-seven are listed as machine-gun dealers, with eleven of those selling silencers. And fifty-two market tear-gas weapons of one sort or another.

"A few things should be pointed out," Hoy comments in his introduction. "First it would not surprise me to learn that just about every weapon in this book is illegal somewhere or other. You are advised to check with your local law enforcement authorities . . . We are not advocating that you use any of this stuff—we just thought you would like to know about it."

What would a well-balanced citizen want with most of these devices? Hoy offers a quote from A. E. van Vogt's science fiction novel, *The Weapon Shops of Isher:* "The right to buy arms," he says piously, "is the right to be free."

You can get a copy of *Exotic Weapons* from Loompanics Unlimited, Box 1197, Port Townsend, WA 98368.

NANNY AT
THE STAKE

Centuries have elapsed since those convicted of practicing the ancient art of witchcraft, namely witches, were routinely burned at the stake. In Italy though, one court seems to have resurrected witchcraft as a modern day crime.

It all began in 1982 when Scotswoman Carole Compton took a job as a nanny with a family on the Italian island of Elba. Almost immediately a pair of suspicious fires started in the family's home, one nearly injuring a sleeping three-year-old girl.

"You've got the devil inside you," the girl's grandmother told Compton. The next thing she knew, Compton says, she was charged with arson and attempted murder. The authorities threw her in jail, where she languished for months.

At trial in Livorno, Italy, witnesses testified that Compton had willed a vase to fly, that electrical meters spun crazily when she walked by, and that she ignited the suspicious fires with the power of her mind. "The family's maid said I turned a key in a lock without touching it," Compton recalls. "I felt like I was in a witch trial out of history."

Indeed many European newspapers bannered "Witch Trial" headlines. But the *coup de grace* came when one of the judges asked Compton if, as alleged, she possessed supernatural powers. Compton says, "I told the judge that if I did, I could open my cell with mind power and escape."

Found guilty of arson last December, the one-time nanny, who had already been jailed for seventeen months, was freed.

Now back in Scotland, Compton (who had no previous criminal record) proclaims her innocence.

Much like the Cheshire Cat, UFOs may appear
spontaneously within a limited area.

UFO UPDATE: DEBATE

E ditor's note: J. Allen Hynek, director of the Center for UFO Studies in Evanston, Illinois, and a leading proponent of the scientific investigation of such phenomena, debates UFO skeptic James Oberg on the meaning of unidentified flying objects.

Hynek:

> "The UFO may
> be an interface between
> our reality
> and a parallel reality."

Close Encounters of the Third Kind and *E.T.* suggest that UFOs are space vehicles piloted by extraterrestrials. This simplistic solution to the UFO problem is summarily rejected by most physical scientists—and with good reason: Even the most sophisticated propulsion devices could not cover the astronomical distances involved in any reasonable length of time. In addition our sophisticated surveillance systems have yet to detect any UFOs approaching or departing from Earth.

And having come from vast distances, UFOs make such poor use of their short visits. So unlike us! We would land prominently, bearing gifts and papers to establish our credibility. They favor lonely roads, late-night hours, and few witnesses.

Though these factors argue against an extraterrestrial explanation, they do not demolish the reality of the UFO phenomenon. UFO sightings continue to be reported from all over the world by military and commercial pilots, engineers, technicians, and other people judged sane and responsible. UFOs just won't go away.

The inconsistency of the situation of course begs some questions: Why are there UFO reports in the first place? Why not reports of pink elephants, for instance, or fiery dragons? What sorts of people make UFO reports? Under what conditions were the UFO sightings made? And how can we explain UFO photographs, inexplicable radar blips, and other bits of physical evidence?

The questions are so diverse that research could be conducted by any number of professionals: physicists, astronomers, sociologists, psychiatrists, or theologians.

The best person to investigate these questions, however, might be the ufologist—someone who applies his particular expertise to the study not of UFOs (we have none in captivity) but to the myriad reports of UFO encounters.

As far as I'm concerned, studying such reports may open a whole new arena of which we are only dimly aware. The key to this alternate reality might lie in the ephemeral nature of UFOs. Much like the Cheshire Cat in *Alice's Adventures in Wonderland,* UFOs appear spontaneously within a limited area, remain visible for a short time, and then disappear without a trace.

This peculiar behavior reminds us of the duality of light, which acts either as a wave or a particle, depending on the particular situation.

Can the UFO likewise have two aspects? Can it be an interface between our reality and a parallel reality, the door to another dimension? Surely we haven't had our last revolution in scientific thought; twenty-first-, twenty-fifth-, or thirtieth-century science may well hold concepts as unintelligible to us as nuclear energy would have been to the caveman.

Oberg:

> "We can account
> for decades of UFO sightings
> without resorting
> to supernatural explanations."

J. Allen Hynek says that intergalactic travel is physically impossible, arguing that UFOs could *not* be craft carrying emissaries from space. Instead he suggests that unidentified flying objects may represent an alternate reality, or even "doors" connecting our universe to some parallel dimension.

I would like to counter that theory with the "null hypothesis," which holds that we can account for decades of UFO sightings without resorting to extraordinary explanations. Under this hypothesis, put forth by skeptical UFO theoretician Robert Sheaffer, there would still be innumerable UFO reports, including some seemingly unexplainable cases. There would still be hypnotically extracted stories of abductions by flying-saucer beings. There would be close encounters of the first, second, and third kind.

There just wouldn't be any UFOs.

Proof of this hypothesis lies in a simple thought experiment. Ufologists now claim that of all UFO reports, 90 percent can be explained, while 10 percent are "true" UFOs. But imagine that all true UFOs go away for a period of time, leaving the UFO reports caused by readily explainable misperceptions, pranks, and hoaxes. Since it is unreasonable to expect amateur UFO investigators to solve all such prosaic cases, we would be left with a residue of false UFO cases, indistinguishable from what pro-UFO investigators present as true UFOs. The obvious implication is that the real world doesn't have real UFOs after all.

Ufologists such as Hynek refute this argument by pointing to the credentials of witnesses. But witnesses need not be drunk, uneducated, myopic, hysterical, or psychotic to succumb to limitations in human perception and memory. In fact studies suggest that the better educated an individual is, the more likely he or she is to fill in the blanks unconsciously.

An excellent example is a set of cases endorsed by Hynek himself. Astronomers in the Caucasus and Volga regions of the U.S.S.R. reported sighting UFOs throughout 1967. The men were actually seeing tests of space-to-Earth orbital thermonuclear warheads, but their reports were interpreted by leading American ufologists as proof that even highly educated people see UFOs.

Until pro-UFO researchers grapple with the reality of human perception and self-deception, alternate universes and interdimensional communication are destined to remain hypotheses in search of data.

Maybe alien starfaring civilizations who *have* mastered the secrets of intergalactic travel are observing our planet. Such beings would, in Arthur C. Clarke's words, be capable of feats "indistinguishable from magic" and could thus conceal themselves from us. Having done so, they may even now be searching for the identity of the UFO pilots, since they know it isn't they!

"We need utopias. Without utopias the world would not change."

—*Thornton Wilder*

Man with groceries: Is he a member of the Breatharian Society?

EATING
AIR

He eats air, sleeps a few hours a week, and lifts ten times his weight. Who is this wonder man? If you believe a recent advertisement, he's Wiley Brooks, founder of the Breatharian Institute of America, based in mellow Marin County, California.

Brooks, author of the book *Breathe and Live Forever,* says he derives all his nourishment from air and cosmic rays. The breatharian philosophy, he adds, is a throwback to ancient times, "when man condensed air into solid and liquid nutrients." Ordinary food deposits poison in the body, he explains, and the result is death.

To spread the word, Brooks currently gives one-day seminars (cost: one hundred dollars), in which students are taught to make the transition from carnivorousness to vegetarianism, fruitarianism, liquidarianism, and finally, breatharianism. No restrooms are provided for advanced students, Brooks notes, since, "if nothing's going in, nothing's coming out."

Though Brooks admits to occasionally imbibing orange juice, he emphasizes, "It's only to cleanse the system of all the pollutants one encounters when living near a city." Some of his former associates, however, claim that breatharianism is a sham and that Brooks is in fact a secret "sugar addict and junk-food junkie." He has reportedly been caught eating a chicken pot pie and was seen leaving a food store with a bag full of groceries. Brooks himself denies these accusations, claiming they were perpetrated by his jealous ex-girlfriend.

Since it's alleged that none of the institute's disciples have ever stopped eating, however, Brooks may be the only "true breatharian" in the world.

"If poltergeist phenomena say anything, I suspect that this is not about spirits, demons, or ghosts but about human personality."

—*William G. Roll*

REVENGE OF THE NEEDLEFISH

Dr. Peter Barss had been at the Milne Bay Hospital in Papua, New Guinea, for just a week when some villagers found the body of a dead fisherman. The young doctor's autopsy revealed a sharp piece of bone (the tip of a crude knife, perhaps?) lodged in the man's chest. A week later villagers found another dead fisherman, and this time Barss discovered the culprit: a thin, silvery fish, alive and kicking deep inside the man's stomach.

After several similar incidents, Barss finally realized that the fishermen were being massacred by foot-long predators called needlefish. The streamlined fish leap from the water at great speed, Barss claims, and literally stab the fishermen with three-inch-long, bony snouts.

"Though most people think the shark is the most dangerous fish in the ocean," says Barss, "it kills only about ten people a year worldwide. The needlefish, however, takes more than twenty lives a month." In one week, he adds, four fishermen died of stab wounds to the chest or stomach, three were blinded in one eye, and two were knocked unconscious.

Since most people have been attacked at night while using lanterns, some doctors suspect the fish leap for the light like moths, striking their victims accidentally. But Barss says this explanation may be inadequate: It does not, for instance, account for the three-year-old girl who was paralyzed after an attack in broad daylight. The villagers, in fact, believe the fish have begun a holy war. Tired of being yanked from their home, they've decided to even the score. The locals, Barss reports, have even begun chanting incantations, calling upon the magical "forces of righteousness" to save them from the briny thugs.

Barss, however, hopes the attacks don't get too much publicity. That, he says, might cause fishermen everywhere to outman and outgun the fish to the point of extinction. "That would be a shame," says Barss, "because needlefish are still very nice to eat."

BANK-ROBBERY DIET

In June 1981 Ronald Springston, thirty, walked into a small bank near his home in rural Wheeler, Arkansas, drew a pistol, and politely instructed the bank teller to pile money in a blue nylon bag. Springston drove off with the bank janitor's car and $8,000 in stolen cash.

Arrested several days later, he claimed that the holdup pistol had been empty and that, incredible as it may sound, hypnotic weight-loss therapy administered two weeks before the crime was responsible for his conduct. It seems Springston was fifty pounds overweight and had tried hypnotism to break his eating habit. The hypnotist put Springston under, then allegedly told him he had the self-confidence to diet or even to rob a bank. Springston began to shed pounds but pulled the bank heist too.

Springston's attorney, W. B. Putman, argued that the rob-a-bank bit was part of the hypnotist's "regular patter." Springston couldn't get the hypnotic suggestion "out of his mind. It kept building and building, and obsession became compulsion." Springston, Putman said, was also an epileptic, and that made him exceptionally susceptible to hypnotic suggestion.

Despite the clever defense, jurors failed to reach a verdict. Rather than face a new trial, Springston bargained for a lenient sentence, serving four months and ten days as a model prisoner at a federal correctional facility. He was released about a year ago.

Springston found prison conducive to dieting, and he notes, "I lost fifty-one pounds while there."

AQUATIC APE

The remarkable features that set humankind apart from the apes can be explained by a watery detour along the course of evolution. That at least is the opinion of British author Elaine Morgan, who says that somewhere between 3.5 and 9 million years ago, our ancestors took to the oceans and there began a long series of aquatic adaptations. When they re-emerged to live on land, their bodies were already "naked" compared to other apes; and their hind legs, grown long and strong from eons of swimming, were ready to assume all the work of walking. Man did not lose his hair because of the need to run while hunting in the sweltering heat of the open savanna, argues Morgan (whose new book *The Aquatic Ape* was recently published in the United States by Stein and Day). If that were the case, the lion and the hyena would surely have lost their hair as well. Instead, she contends, man lost his hair for the same reason the whale and the dolphin lost theirs: "Because if any fairly large aquatic mammal needs to keep warm in water, it is better served by a layer of fat on the inside of its skin than by a layer of hair on the outside of it."

Speech would not have emerged as an aid to the hunt, either, Morgan continues, adding that primitive tribes surviving today hunt in silence despite their rich heritage of language. More likely speech became essential to protoman when the need to swim and dive cut down on eye-to-eye contact, making facial expressions difficult to read.

Morgan also notes that while human tears distinguish our species as "the weeping primate," seals and other sea mammals cry as well. "If we view man as a land animal," she says, "he is unique and inexplicable. If we view him as an ex-aquatic, he is conforming to the general pattern."

In the absence of fossil evidence for the missing link, contends Morgan, the aquatic theory makes as much sense as other arguments formulated to fill the gap.

BLOODSCOPES

In Japan, the question "What's your blood type?" is quickly replacing "What's your sign?" The reason: a fifty-year-old book entitled *Blood Groups and Temperatures* by psychologist Takeji Furukawas. According to Furukawas, people with type O blood are the best employees; type B's are flexible, freedom-loving people; and type A's flourish in structured environments.

Though medical authorities dismissed the book years ago, Japanese interest in blood types is reaching fad proportions. The craze, according to the Japanese Red Cross, has doubled the number of blood donors in the sixteen- to nineteen-year-old age bracket—young people are flocking to bloodmobiles to find out what type blood they have. A Japanese matchmaking service requests that clients list their blood types, and a Japanese polling institute reports blood types among the demographic factors it surveys. "Bloodscopes," or blood-type-based horoscopes, are even running in several women's magazines.

Combating Furukawas' resurgence, officials in Japan and elsewhere continue to debunk his work. Suguru Akaishi, director of the Japan Red Cross Center in Miyagi Prefecture, says, "Human psychology just isn't so simple that it can be determined by blood types." And Charles Huguley, head of Emory University's Hematology Department adds, "I've never heard of any scientific findings tying blood type to personality."

Siberian scientists have been eating mammoth meat
frozen and preserved thousands of years ago.

MAMMOTH
BURGERS

Next time you visit Siberia, you might be offered some exotic culinary fare: mammoth meat, roasted or fried.

The mammoth, that hairy ancestor of today's elephant, has been presumed extinct for thousands of years. But people have reportedly eaten the animal's frozen remains for centuries. During the 1920s tourists visiting Siberia claimed they feasted on mammoth flesh. It's been rumored that Russian scientists occasionally gather for "mammoth banquets." And just recently a group of Soviet construction workers caused a stir among paleontologists by preparing mammoth meat for their dogs.

The issue came to a head at a recent Helsinki symposium on mammoth tissue. Some researchers suggested that mammoths may still be roaming the Siberian plains. And zoologist Nikolai Vereshchagin, of the Soviet Academy of Sciences, even proposed cloning a new mammoth herd from a few frozen cells.

American researchers who examined the frozen mammoth tissue, however, cast doubt on such plans. Paleontologist David Webb, of the Florida State Museum in Gainesville, for instance, found the flesh was poorly preserved. "By and large," Webb said, "the specimens were about fifty percent sludge and fifty percent real cells, and the chance of cloning them is pretty slim with today's technology."

Eating the disintegrating flesh may not be too good an idea, either. Geologist Robert M. Thorson of the University of Alaska in Fairbanks is presently excavating a local, partially preserved mammoth. Though he hasn't had the chance to taste mammoth meat, he did sample the flesh of a bison found in permafrost sediments some 30,000 years old. "The piece I ate tasted pretty bad," Thorson says. Colleagues who ate mammoth meat also found the quality left a lot to be desired, he adds. But at least nobody's gotten sick.

Troubled psychic:
Now there's a hotline
she can call for help.

SPIRITUAL
EMERGENCY
NETWORK

While meditating, a young woman recalls being entombed alive during a previous life. This sudden jarring of her subconscious mind has triggered mood swings from depression to hysteria.

Most psychiatrists would label her psychotic, recommending a hospital stay, drugs, or both. But according to Stanislav Grof, M.D., resident scholar at California's Esalen Institute, such a diagnosis would be a grave mistake. The young woman, he says, is actually in the midst of a "spiritual emergency," a frequent consequence of death and rebirth, past-life recall, and ESP.

To provide the stricken with appropriate care, Grof and his wife, Christina, have recently founded the Spiritual Emergency Network (SEN). The network has already recruited sympathetic psychologists, theologists, and spiritualists to assist its patients. And in just three years, the group has grown from a phone line in Big Sur to a twenty-four-hour referral service, with on-call counselors in thirty-two countries. Workers are currently organizing retreats for long-term care.

SEN asks troubled ESPers and past-lifers, as well as potential counselors, to call the network at (408) 667-2151.

CHOPPER'S GHOST

Dentist Kurt Bachseitz, of Neutraubling, West Germany, was arranging an appointment with a patient on the phone recently when a voice blurted out, "You needn't bother going. It won't do the slightest good."

The voice, often wisecracking and insolent, was heard time and time again over the coming months. The phone company was called on for assistance and, suspecting some kind of electronic interference from a ham radio operator, checked the system thoroughly. Then it installed a new line and relaid all the telephone cable in the dentist's office building.

But nothing worked. The voice, which took to calling itself Chopper, had developed a soft spot for the dentist's seventeen-year-old receptionist, Claudia. "I love you, Claudia," it told her. Soon it was projecting from the washbasin, the spittoon, and even, to the acute embarrassment of one patient, the toilet.

The ghost's voice was even played over a Munich radio station for all Bavaria to hear. "You've taken away my switchboard," Chopper complained. "But I can hear you just as well. So don't think I'm not listening in!" Soon the ghost was in all the newspapers, and all manner of explanations were put forth.

A parapsychologist said the voice was definitely a paranormal phenomenon. A philosophy professor proposed that the voice was a ghostly manifestation of the unconscious. And doctors suggested it was produced by a cancer patient whose vocal cords had been lost to surgery.

Then, a while after it all began, Claudia confessed: The ghost was the dentist, who was a skilled ventriloquist. It was a practical joke, Claudia said, that had simply got out of hand.

Soon thereafter, the dentist closed his office and entered a sanatorium, perhaps to escape a possible phone company bill for 60,000 Marks.

Vulture in flight: These vicious scavengers still haunt
the battlefield at Gettysburg.

VULTURES
OF GETTYSBURG

Each winter hundreds of vultures descend on the cannons and monuments of Gettysburg National Military Park. The carrion-eating birds—labeled by myth and history as sentinels of death—roost amid the grapevines, and their droppings cover the ground like a heavy dusting of snow.

Black vultures and turkey vultures, says park resource specialist Harold J. Greenlee, have been visiting the Pennsylvania site for at least a century. But now Greenlee and colleagues have launched a study to find out why. The group's prime theory: The birds were attracted to the area on July 1, 1863, after the start of one of the bloodiest battles of the Civil War.

After three days of fighting, says Greenlee, Plum Run, a small stream that flows through the battlefield, ran red with blood. Nearly 50,000 men lay slaughtered or dying. And thousands of dead horses covered the ground for months. "The birds roost on Little Round Top and Big Round Top, hills where some of the heaviest battles took place," he explains. "So it's not unreasonable that the vultures could have been attracted to the bodies; they might have scavenged the horse carcasses, stayed on for the winter, and then gotten into the habit of coming here."

Greenlee is currently working with students and professors from Virginia Polytechnic Institute and Pennsylvania State University to study the vultures' habitat, as well as their migration and feeding patterns. "We want to explain to the public," says Greenlee, "why nine hundred vultures continue to roost in a national park."

Disembodied head:
It wasn't hostile,
just playful and young.

"He dashed to the
bathroom, splashed cold water on
his face, and shot
the specters with his Polaroid One-Step."

UFO UPDATE

It isn't that Rev. Harrison E. Bailey minds taking dictation. But when he was stirred at 1:30 A.M. to record the word of two disembodied heads, he started to shake. Bailey's incredible tale is enough to shake just about anyone.

The preacher says he awoke early on the morning of November 1, 1978, to find a couple of ghostlike aliens against the window shade of his Pasadena, California, apartment. He dashed to the bathroom, splashed cold water on his face, and returned to shoot the dark brown specters with his trusty Polaroid One-Step.

Then came the message, a half hour of religious generalities. Stenography isn't the former steelworker's best skill, yet Bailey managed to get it all down—including the final "I love you," repeated ten times in Chinese, a language he does not speak.

To help the clergyman prove his story, the aliens sat for more photos, growing wizened, whitish legs for the full-length portraits. They also donned

175

Halloween masks that Bailey had saved from a party. It made them look a bit less authentic, but the minister took five pictures anyway.

Suddenly, Bailey says, the aliens darted toward the bathroom, their shapes now humanoid and four feet tall. He got a photo of each in the hallway, then glimpsed them shooting through the ceiling in whirling globes of light.

Bailey returned to bed and dreamed fitfully of his strange visitors. After fretting for more than two months, he told his tale to his friend and longtime ufologist Ann Druffel, who passed the pictures to psychic researchers for criticism and analysis.

As might be expected, the photos got mixed reviews. Cyril Permutt of the Bureau for the Investigation of Paranormal Photographs in London has reported that they "showed no trace of a hoax."

One Los Angeles ufologist, however, announced: "These photos are an embarrassment. The entities might be made from stockings." Some of the photos were puzzling even to Druffel. "The photos with the masks," she says, "seem to have been taken with a flash, yet Bailey says he didn't use one." She offers what she feels is a logical explanation, though: "I think the light source was paranormal."

The beings disrupted Bailey's sleep for years. Then, on Halloween, 1982, he asked Druffel and psychic Anita Furdek to exorcise the creatures. As Druffel and Furdek tell it, it was a hard battle: Furdek was tossed all night as though racked by epileptic seizures. The creatures weren't hostile, Furdek feels, just playful and young.

At 5 A.M. Furdek finally persuaded them to leave Bailey in peace, then went downstairs to discover that Druffel's car had been stolen. "I looked out the window," Furdek says, "to see the E.T.'s having the last laugh."

It's a strange tale, Druffel admits. But she says, "Most of the researchers who meet Bailey feel he is extremely rational and honest. We just have to accept his word, because he has been unable to duplicate this effect in front of scientists."

"History is more or less bunk."

—*Henry Ford*

Giant cloud: If it reaches Earth, it could cause another ice age.

THE CLOUD
IS COMING

After many arduous years of telescope gazing, a group of French astronomers has discovered to their dismay a giant interstellar cloud heading directly toward the planet Earth from the direction of the constellation Sagittarius.

Some climatologists believe the passage of dense interstellar clouds through our solar system could cause ice ages; others say such clouds could render the sun more luminous. But, whichever way it goes, warns astronomer Alfred Vidal-Madjar and his colleagues at the Laboratory for Stellar and Planetary Physics, in Verrières-le-Buisson, the presence of a nearby cloud could have "some drastic influence on the terrestrial climate sometime during the next ten thousand years."

Direct observation of the interstellar medium is a very tricky business, says Vidal-Madjar. Nonetheless his group's results have been confirmed by at least two other astronomers working independently. "This is the strongest evidence yet," he says, "in favor of the cloud."

The gaseous interloper may be roughly cigar-shaped, Vidal-Madjar says, and perhaps ten times longer than its 0.33-light-year thickness. Traveling toward Earth from Sagittarius at the speed of about 15 to 20 kilometers per second, it might well be 0.1 light-year from Earth by now. If so, it will be here in about 1,500 years. But the data are just too skimpy for precise predictions, and Vidal-Madjar admits there's a remote chance that the cloud is no farther from Earth than the sun is. At that distance it would arrive by the year 2001.

These two young men are walking upside down for the Lord.

THE HANDSTAND TWINS

Ron and Richard Bowser were abandoned at birth and left on the floor of a cabin in the woods. They were found near death, their vocal cords damaged and their bones malformed; one doctor even said they might be retarded. The twins felt unloved by their foster parents throughout childhood, and Ron tried killing himself twice by the age of fifteen.

But when the pair turned sixteen, things started looking up: They began weightlifting, and before long Ron won the Mr. Teenage Pennsylvania bodybuilding contest, going on to become a nationally ranked weightlifter. After being discharged from the Marines, he attended college for a year and then joined Richard, who was working in a steel mill. Two years later Ron fell to his knees and "asked Jesus to enter my heart." Within a year both Bowsers were ordained ministers. Shortly thereafter they worked out a performance routine that consisted of walking on their hands. For a fee the Bowsers today preach, sing, and do handstand balancing acts in churches all across the country.

"We're the only set of identical twins in the world who walk upside down for the Lord," says Ron. Notes Richard, "Nobody's walked down as many steps on their hands as we have."

The twins also march in parades. One walks on his hands; the other follows, wheeling a ten-foot cross with splotches of red paint on it. "One guy yelled to us that Jesus didn't use a wheel," says Ron. Adds Richard, "So we told him we'd take off the wheel if he'd accept Jesus into his heart."

At another parade Richard found himself staring down a shotgun barrel held by a man ordering him to drop the cross. "I rendered his powers impotent in the name of Jesus, and he dropped the gun and ran," he says. "But it's not something you want to try all the time."

The Bowsers also have a dream: They'd like to walk on their hands down the steps of the Empire State Building, the Washington Monument, and yet-to-be-announced structures throughout Paris, London, Rome, and Asia. "Our motto," says Richard, "is that if we can walk for Him upside down, you can walk for Him right side up."

The Hebrew Bible used words such as "power"
and "equal" to describe Eve.

"Everything clever has already been thought;
we must try to think it again."

—*Johann Wolfgang*
von Goethe

EQUALITY
FOR EVE

Those who insist that a woman's place is in
the home frequently back up their beliefs
with the biblical story of Genesis. The Bible, they say, clearly states that woman
was created as a helpmate for man. Wrong, says religion-archaeology-language
scholar David Freedman.

Freedman, who is Director of Religious Studies at the University of California at Davis, explains that the Hebrew word *ezer* is usually translated in
Genesis as "helper" or "helpmate." But the word should actually be interpreted as "a power" or "a strength." And *kenegdo,* which is usually read as
meaning "fit," actually means "equal." Thus Genesis says that woman was
created as "a power equal to man" instead of as "a helper fit for man."

If you go back to the earliest Jewish writing, says Freedman, the meaning
is clear. "But so many translations have been influenced by the King James
version of the Bible, in which the Genesis passage is misinterpreted, that things
get fixed in people's minds."

> "Scientists who
> search for extraterrestrials
> are driven by the
> need for religious salvation."

UFO
UPDATE

At 9 A.M. it is still pitch-black in the Soviet city of Tallinn. Just across the Gulf of Finland lies Helsinki and due north the Arctic. On this particular day hundreds of people forge through frigid winds and blustering snow to attend a meeting at the sports complex. After removing their parkas and furs, arrivals sit, eyes darting with excitement, and listen to members of their group, including the tall, fair-haired V. S. Troitsky. "The search for extraterrestrial intelligence is a problem facing the whole of mankind," he declares. "It is of great scientific, philosophical, and social significance." When he concludes, the applause is swift and resounding.

Does this seem like some UFO cult in the depths of the U.S.S.R.? Maybe, but the convention, held a few years ago, drew dozens of the world's most prominent astronomers, four cosmonauts, and a member of the Supreme Soviet. Troitsky is a shining light of Soviet science.

One contrary physicist, Frank Tipler of Tulane University in New Orleans, was not impressed. Scientists who believe in extraterrestrial intelligence (ETI) live in a world of fantasy, he claims. What motivates them? "The hope of semireligious salvation." Why else, Tipler asks, would Carl Sagan of "Cosmos" fame assert that extraterrestrials might send us "prescriptions for the avoidance of technological disaster"? Why would Frank Drake of Cornell University in Ithaca, New York, say, "We can expect [the immortals] to spread the secret of their immortality among us"?

While Sagan, Drake, and others use complex equations to show there's a high probability of intelligent life out there, Tipler says, "Hogwash." Any civilization slightly more advanced than ours, he explains, would already have colonized the galaxy, including Earth, with their own version of the Von Neumann machine—the space-traveling robot dreamed up by mathematician John von Neumann.

Programmed to search for life, the Von Neumann machine would leave its home planet for a nearby world rich in minerals and fuels. Using available substances, the machine could build a dozen copies of itself, sending each to a different sector of the cosmos. Each copy could then make more until, 300 million years hence, the probes would have traversed the universe. "The oldest stars are eighteen billion years old, so their inhabitants have had plenty of time to arrive," Tipler asserts. "Since they are not here, obviously they do not exist."

Despite the supreme logic of this argument, Tipler says, ETI advocates, led by Sagan, have unwittingly conspired to prevent him from expressing his views. His proof: Two American journals, *Science* and *Icarus,* refused to publish his story. In both cases, he charges, Sagan influenced their decision. To Tipler that is not surprising. "A characteristic of religious motivation," he says, "is the inability to consider an antireligious argument dispassionately."

Sagan, however, emphasizes that in both cases he "was only one of several referees. I was in no position to *prevent* publication," he adds, "only to advise against it."

ROBOTS
FOR THE DEAD

A family attends the funeral of a dearly loved relative, then returns home to find him sitting in his favorite chair, chatting just as he used to.

This scenario was conceived by psychologist Neil Frude, of University College in Cardiff, Wales. The bereaved, says Frude, will one day reap sustenance from life-size robots that are moving and talking replicas of their dead relatives; the robots will be programmed to talk the same way, make the same gestures, and physically interact with their owners.

In recent years, Frude observes, the dying have made videotaped messages for their loved ones, who screen the tapes time and again in a desperate attempt to maintain the fiction that their nearest and dearest are still alive. The sort of person who leaves video testaments, Frude adds, would probably welcome the chance of "bequeathing an electronic double encased in a look-alike vinyl shell. He could make a bid for something akin to immortality by ordering a computerized automaton in his own image, matching its values, opinions, and preference to his own."

Frude admits that the idea of a bereaved person conversing with a plastic model of a dead relative is "profoundly disturbing." But such weird relationships, he says in his new book, *The Intimate Machine,* might well arise to satisfy human needs.

Baby Darling: She speaks Spanish too.

"Don't let your mind be cluttered up with prevailing doctrine."

—*Alexander Fleming*

KILL MOMMY DOLLS

Ruby Smith, of Walhalla, South Carolina, recently purchased a golden-haired talking doll for her eight-year-old daughter. But when Ruby pulled the string that activated the doll's recorded voice, she was shocked to hear Baby Darling say, "Kill our Mommy." Outraged, she quickly contacted the Greenville Better Business Bureau.

"We received several complaints from upset customers who had purchased the dolls," Carla Cox, the bureau's operations manager, reported. "We also heard from our Chicago office that a 'Kill Mommy' doll had shown up there."

Disturbed by the reports, those who distributed Baby Darling dolls, manufactured in Hong Kong, began seeking an explanation. Frank Berkley, of Bits and Pieces—a Gastonia, North Carolina, company—suggested that the dolls were actually saying, "Kim Loves Mommy." When the mechanism slowed, he claimed the voice deepened, making the phrase sound like "Kill our Mommy."

It was Stuart Sankel, a distributor in Miami, however, who hit upon the real explanation: The doll wasn't demanding matricide at all. Instead it was simply saying *"Quiero mami,"* Spanish for "I love Mommy." In Miami, where over 500,000 Spanish-speaking people live, in fact, the Baby Darling dolls were accepted without question.

"I met with the manufacturer," Sankel stated, "and he told me he had inadvertently distributed more Spanish-speaking dolls than he meant to."

Carla Cox agrees that there was no sinister plot connected to the purported murderous utterings of Baby Darling. "My neighbor is from Honduras, and he immediately recognized the phrase as Spanish," she says, "but if you don't speak Spanish, it sure does sound like 'Kill our Mommy.' It's no wonder parents were shocked."

MERPEOPLE
OF NEW GUINEA

The Nakela clan of New Guinea was performing a ritual mourning dance when the drummer made a mistake. Members of the troupe were so humiliated, they jumped off a high sea cliff. Their bodies turned to rocks that can still be seen, and their souls became mermaids and mermen, or *ri.*

This ancient tale is only a myth. But if anthropologist Roy Wagner of the University of Virginia is correct, part of the haunting legend may actually be true. Wagner claims that dozens of New Guinea natives may have *seen* the merpeople—creatures with human heads and torsos and legless lower trunks terminating in fins.

Wagner first heard of the *ri* in 1979, when an elderly New Guinea man mentioned the terror of a merperson cast upon a beach decades before. Intrigued, the anthropologist went on to "interview everyone who claimed to have encounters with the creature." One man reported a teenage girl *ri* caught in a net by a native fisherman. A ten-year-old boy described a line of male and female *ri* swimming into a freshwater stream by moonlight. And others mentioned that fishermen sometimes butcher *ri,* then sell the tasty flesh on the open market.

Eyewitness descriptions of *ri* vary considerably, Wagner reports, though most concur on the basic points: The upper torso of the creature is human or humanlike, with long, dark head hair and relatively light skin. The females have obvious mammalian breasts, and each sex has humanlike genitals on the front of the lower torso. Fingernails are long and sharp, the palms are ridged and calloused, and there is something strange about the mouth. They breathe air, they live off fish, and they aren't known to speak.

When questioned about the report, biologist Roy Mackal, of the University of Chicago, said, "A real mermaid—half fish and half human—is genetically impossible. But the creatures could be an unknown sirenian, the group of mammalian species that includes dugongs and manatees. It's even possible, though highly improbable, that *ri* are a genetically defective, inbred group of humans. Because of the anecdotal nature of the evidence, though, it's really difficult to hazard a guess."

Wagner himself concedes that "from an anatomical and evolutionary perspective, the *ri* does pose problems. But," he insists, "the credibility of some of my informants can't be lightly dismissed."

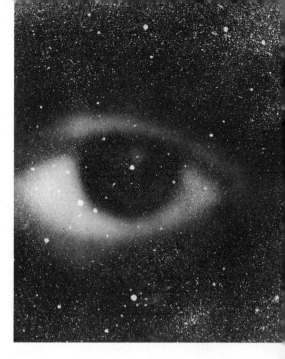

Eye in the sky:
Aliens have made it
possible to photograph
the eye of God.

"Meier met
Jesus Christ and shot an
out-of-focus
photo of the eye of God."

UFO UPDATE

Rouged and radiant, blue-eyed, voluptuous, and blond, she could leap out from the pages of *Vogue*. She's as torrid a number now as she was a century ago. Her name is Semjase, and if you believe a Swiss farmer named Eduard "Billy" Meier, she is a three-hundred-year-old emissary from the Pleiades star cluster.

Semjase and four other Pleiadean cosmonauts, says Meier, have been visiting him in their flying saucers since 1975; they've even taken him for jaunts into the past and through the universe. Semjase once introduced him to Jesus Christ, who made Meier his fourteenth disciple. On another occasion Meier shot an out-of-focus photo of the eye of God. And in July of 1975 he snapped a close-up of the *Apollo* and *Soyuz* capsules linking up in orbit.

Meier has taken so many pictures, in fact, that a group called Genesis III Productions, headed by retired U.S. Air Force Lieutenant Colonel Wendelle C. Stevens, has compiled two books of them. Most of the shots show saucers

187

soaring above trees and meadows, with the Swiss hills undulating in the distance. According to Stevens, Genesis III had the photos analyzed by NASA scientists, who could find no traces whatsoever of a hoax; unfortunately, Stevens adds, "the researchers asked not to be identified."

UFO experts, however, claim the photos are bogus. Jim Lorenzen, of the Aerial Phenomena Research Organization, says he can prove the saucers in the photo are eighteen-inch models. Bill Spaulding, of Ground Saucer Watch, analyzed the photos by computer, finding double exposures (saucers superimposed on meadows) in some and string holding up the saucers in others. Kal Korff, author of *The Meier Incident: Most Infamous Hoax in Ufology*, says witnesses have discovered flying-saucer models on Meier's clothesline, as well as film negatives of models lying half burned in Meier's garbage can. "The eye-of-God photo," adds Korff, "was clearly a blurred shot of the Ring Nebula in the constellation Lyra. And the Apollo-Soyuz photograph was obviously taken directly off a television screen; it didn't even show the actual space capsules, just simulations that had been given to the networks by NASA."

None of this, however, has stopped people from believing Meier. He's sold photos and articles throughout Europe and the United States, and a full-blown cult has formed around him. The believers, who call themselves the Semjase Silver Star Center, live with Meier on a communal farm, providing him with funds and shelter. "When I met him," says Stevens, "he and his family were living on a dirt floor in a chicken coop. Now he has a nice apartment, a TV, and an IBM Selectric typewriter."

Some people hint that Meier has enjoyed other benefits. During those intergalactic voyages, they say, he and the stunning Semjase became romantically involved. "That's ridiculous," scoffs Stevens. "Pleiadeans really don't like humans; we carry too much lust and greed in our aura. Semjase told Meier that making love to him would be like rolling around with pigs."

"What counts is
communicating the
indispensable, skipping all
the superfluous, reducing
ourselves . . . to a luminous
signal that moves in a
given direction."

—*Italo Calvino*

Chicken hearts: Los Angeles cabinetmaker Edward Stewart tries to make them beat with plant juice.

FRANKENSTEIN IN L.A.

Los Angeles cabinetmaker Edward Stewart may be a modern-day Dr. Frankenstein. In 1959 he claims he restored a dead friend to life with a simple technique: He opened the man's chest, rubbed his heart with a "secret, life-giving" plant juice, then stimulated the heartbeat with 110 volts of electricity. The friend, says Stewart, has been sipping piña coladas in Hawaii ever since.

Stewart also claims his revivification technique works on the small animals he suffocates in jars in his garage. It takes three hours to revive a dead mouse, he reports, and five hours for a small dog. "Sometimes," he adds, "I buy those little chicken giblets in the A & P—you know, chicken hearts and gizzards—and I make them beat again using my plant juice before I cook them for dinner."

According to Stewart, he discovered the plant juice one day while trimming hedges around his former home in Hawaii. Sap from one of the tender limbs splattered onto his wrist, he says, and he suddenly noticed the skin begin to twitch. Nonetheless, he adds, he can't reveal the name of the plant. "When the juice is zapped with electricity," he says, "it gives off a deadly gas. I'm afraid the Russians will get it and take over the world."

To promote his idea, Stewart has spent the past decade sending his papers to UCLA, the Army, and a spate of government agencies. One scientist who evaluated the concept was Lynn Eldridge, of the Jerry Lewis Neuromuscular Research Center in Los Angeles. She says Stewart may not be perpetrating a joke. "The extracts from plants like belladonna are used to supply nutrients to human organs, which must be kept alive while en route to a transplant. So Stewart might cut the heart out of a mouse and keep it alive with plant juice. But this effect is short-lived, and the organ must be placed into a healthy body or it dies. It's impossible to place a live organ in a dead body and expect it to revive every other organ in that body. I think Stewart has observed a basic scientific phenomenon, but his interpretation is out there."

Stewart recently discovered he had a cancerous tumor. Though he admits he could leave the instructions for someone to revive him should he die, he still goes for radiation treatments. "If something went wrong with the plant juice," he says, "I wouldn't be around to perfect it and give it to mankind." Besides, he claims, "government investigators are watching my garage. They've told me not to experiment on humans, which is a damn shame."

Some people claim
that statues of
the Virgin Mary
cry real tears.

WEEPING
MADONNA

For the past few years, folks in Thornton, California, have been mystified by a sculpture in the Mater Ecclesia Mission Church.

Some people claimed the sixty-pound statue of the Virgin Mary could move thirty feet from its niche. Others reported that the statue cried real tears. Carlota Usuna of Modesto insisted that she was cured of asthma after praying to the weeping Madonna. And church volunteer Manual Pitta produced color photos that apparently showed the face of Christ floating above the statue in midair.

As tales of these miracles circulated, church attendance tripled, and the local diocese named a panel of priests to study the mystery. The verdict? "A deception was perpetrated," Bishop Roger Mahoney says. "But we don't know why someone would want to do this sort of thing."

Mahoney explains that the Roman Catholic Church validates miracles that are accompanied by clear, important messages. But the weeping Madonna failed to give any such pronouncements. Moreover the oily liquid found on the statue's face didn't resemble human tears, and the statue's shifting could be explained by someone's secretly moving it.

What about the photographs with Christ's head? Charles V. Morton, director of the Institute of Forensic Science Criminalistics Laboratory in Oakland, California, studied the photos and concluded: "The pictures of Jesus were from commercially available religious magazines. In fact, the edges were clearly cut, and in one case there's a crease across the face of Jesus showing where the paper had been folded."

Although the weeping Virgin of Thornton has proved to be a hoax, investigators say there's yet another crying Madonna; this one allegedly oozes fragrant, oily tears as she makes the rounds of Russian Orthodox churches throughout the eastern United States.

Panhandler: He collects money from people visiting the alien's grave.

ALIEN
OF AURORA

By 1897 the railroad taking settlers west had already bypassed Aurora, Texas. The reason: A plague of yellow fever had killed off most of the people, and the place was fast becoming a ghost town. Those who were not in the cemetery prayed for a miracle to attract new settlers, and then it happened.

In the spring of 1897, local newspapers reported that the nose of a "mysterious airship" had struck the water well on Judge J. S. Proctor's farm. The charred body of an alien, reports said, was buried in the cemetery, and a porthole was engraved on the tombstone.

For the past seventy-five years UFO investigators have said the crash was a hoax designed to bring the curious to town. But now Walter Andrus, an investigator for the Mutual UFO Network (MUFON) in Texas, says a piece of the mysterious airship has been found. Modern metallurgical tests, he adds, have proved that whatever crashed wasn't man-made.

Andrus claims that a scrap of metal was found near Proctor's well by

MUFON investigator Bill Case. The metal, he adds, conformed to the shape of the stone in which it was discovered, indicating that it must have been nearly molten as it hurtled down.

More significantly, Andrus contends, an X ray verified the presence of pure aluminum in the sample, "which is meaningful," he explains, "because all known commercial aluminum must contain copper. But this sample did not have copper." Andrus, unfortunately, cannot reveal the name of the laboratory that conducted the test because, he says, "the lab normally charges seventy-five dollars an hour," but his group managed to avoid the fee.

UFO expert James Oberg, however, points out that it doesn't take Sherlock Holmes to realize something's amiss. Since the lab can't be revealed, there is no way to verify the test results, he says. Moreover, "if this is a hoax, the popularity of the town's only tourist attraction would be ruined. You know, there's a guy at the gate of the Aurora cemetery who collects money from people coming to see the alien's grave. Why don't they just dig it up?"

GRASS MAN

If you pass a grass-covered man driving a grass-covered Buick LeSabre, it's probably Bill Harding, a twenty-four-year-old Kansas City artist who's into grass. According to Harding, the grass car is an artistic expression "of the wedding of grass and steel. It's a metaphor for survival," he says, "pointing toward man's need to balance nature and technology."

To grow the grass, Harding spreads a petroleum-based adhesive over his car and clothes. Then he sprays seedlings onto the paste and puts clothes and car into a tent. "The tent," he says, "keeps the objects moist while I water them like crazy, four times a day, singing to the seed as I go so they grow faster, which they do."

Right now, Harding admits, he's most interested in the effect that grass clothes have on the wearer. When a person wears a grass suit, Harding points out, he can feel the roots growing through the fabric. "It's the only instance I know of being encased in a living thing other than the womb," he says. "And I find it makes me very calm."

Harding, in fact, persuaded pro bowler Bob Hendley to bowl wearing a grass suit. The suit didn't improve Hendley's score. But using a galvanic-skin-response machine, Harding found that the bowler's skin registered less nervous energy when he was wearing grass.

One day, Harding predicts, the practical applications of grass garments will be realized. People will wear grass at home after a hard day's work. Football players will wear grass helmets at halftime. And, he adds, astronauts will wear grass in space to remind them of Earth.

Toward that day, Harding has now joined the lecture circuit; donning his grass suit, he speaks in shopping malls all over the United States. Recently, he admits, one skeptic chased him around a Kansas farmers' market for four hours—with a lawn mower.

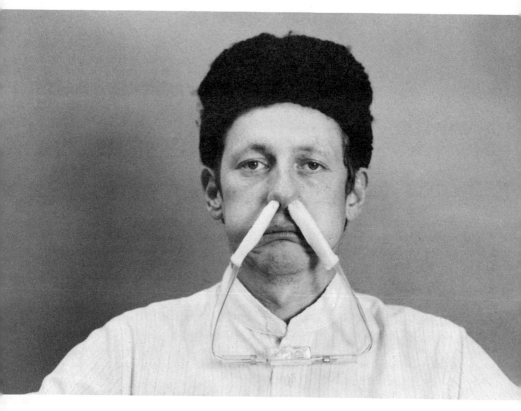

Tampons for the nose: A Soviet researcher says they
can cure the common cold.

"I'm lonely and shy. Women don't like me. Unfortunately, real life is different from movie fiction. I've got many girlfriends, but I still can't find my twin soul. One day, who knows, I might find her amidst the thousands of fans who write or call on me."

—*Richard Chamberlain*

RUSSIAN COLD CURE

Good news from the Soviet Union: According to researcher Yuri Mironenko, the common cold can now be cured. The new treatment is painless, quick, and fairly inexpensive, Mironenko says. But it has one disadvantage: You have to walk around with tampons up your nose.

The tampons are soaked in a silver solution and connected to a conductor worn around the cold sufferer's neck, Mironenko explains in a recent *Lenin Banner* newspaper story. A low current of electricity generated by the conductor supposedly activates silver ions, which rush through the skin, "oppressing the activity of the cold virus." Because it is quite important to keep the viruses "oppressed" until your sniffles are gone, Mironenko adds, the conductor must be recharged often. But not to worry, Mironenko has also invented a handy battery-powered recharger that can be worn in your shirt pocket.

Do American researchers think Soviet science has eradicated the common cold? Not exactly. As Dr. Gary Noble, assistant director for science with the Centers for Disease Control in Atlanta, points out: "If this helps with colds at all, there's probably a simple reason—by plugging up the nose with tampons, you keep the cold viruses from getting down the respiratory tract."

"Kolb abducted his
wife as she left her night job; then
Patrick took her to his
basement and began the deprogramming."

UFO
UPDATE

Ted Patrick is known worldwide as the man who kidnapped and deprogrammed young Moonies from Reverend Moon's Unification Church, where, he contends, they were brainwashed. But most people don't know about Patrick's most recent battle: finding and deprogramming those who had been brainwashed by the country's UFO cults.

Patrick's involvement with UFO cults began at his San Diego home one night in 1979, when he got a surprise visit from Thomas Kolb. Kolb's twenty-four-year-old wife, Susan, it seems, had seen flashing orange lights over their Kiel, Wisconsin, home. Since then, she'd been going to Wisconsin's UFO Education Center, where, Thomas claimed, founder Charlotte Blob (rhymes with *globe)* had brainwashed Susan into thinking that she could save the world.

Blob allegedly told Susan that the late George Adamski, a former center member, had taken flying saucer rides to meet the "Master"; the Master in turn had promised Adamski that his "space brothers" would send telepathic messages teaching center members to purge society of drugs, war, and poverty. Moreover those who saved the world would be reincarnated on Saturn.

Lured by Blob's promises, says Patrick, Susan abandoned Thomas and their three-year-old daughter for a life at the center. Later she took on three jobs to meet the center's required weekly donations of $20 to $30, as well as other expected "spot contributions" of up to $100.

It was at this point that Kolb ended up on Patrick's doorstep and the two concocted a plan. Thomas abducted Susan as she left one of her night jobs at a bank. Then Patrick, who was paid $5,000, led her to a bare room in the basement of his house. He sat her on a stool under a naked light bulb and asked whether she knew that Blob had used center money for private real-estate investments. Susan mumbled no, and Patrick went on, asking whether humans needed space suits to travel to other planets. Susan said yes, and he asked if in three years she had ever seen a space suit. When she said no, he asked her how Adamski could have met the Master without a space suit. "It is possible," he

UFO cult member: She must be deprogrammed if she is to resume normal life.

demanded, "that someone has been lying to you?" The questions went on for days, and finally, Patrick says, he "snapped" Susan back to reality.

Today Susan is home, and Patrick has gone on to deprogram other cultists as well. He saved one twenty-three-year-old who moved into the Wisconsin center after telling her parents: "You don't mean anything more to me than the manure on this earth." He has also succeeded in rescuing elderly members of "Bo and Peep," an underground UFO cult promising golden-agers a flying-saucer ride to Venus and the Fountain of Youth.

Patrick blames the proliferation of UFO cults on movies like *Close Encounters of the Third Kind* and *E.T.,* as well as on the government. With UFO cults around, he says, "it's easier to cover up the real UFOs: new weapons, killer satellites, lasers, and missiles."

ANIMAL
SACRIFICE

There were goats, sheep, roosters, chickens, guinea hens, pigeons, and a duck. And they weren't on Old Macdonald's farm.

The animals, fifty-two in all, were crowded into a Manhattan apartment, most of them in one room, waiting to be the main event in a recent religious sacrifice. That was the report of James Hill, a deputy director of law enforcement for the ASPCA who took a look at the urban abattoir at the request of local police.

Hill was not surprised by what he found. Animal sacrifice may sound like an ancient ritual, but it is an everyday affair in twentieth-century New York City. The sacrifices play a part in the Santeria cult, which had its birth among black slaves brought to Cuba in the eighteenth century. The cult is still healthy in places like New York City and Dade County, Florida, where a retired Miami detective reported witnessing a woman rub her naked body with a chicken, kill it, and throw it in the Miami River as two other women in robes chanted an accompaniment.

Hill said he was "not trying to interfere with anybody's religion," but farm animals were not even *allowed* in Manhattan. In addition some of the prospective sacrifices—the goats—were found "tussled up in very heavy plastic bags. The only thing sticking out was their heads." That, said Hill, constituted cruelty to animals, as would the sacrifice itself.

The ASPCA actually conducted some discussions with representatives of the religious sects a few years ago, but there was little to talk about. Either the law had to change, said Hill, or the cultists had to replace their sacrificial rituals with a peaceful ceremonial practice, "like drinking wine."

In the recent case, Hill issued two summonses to Maria Castro, who lives on Manhattan's Lower East Side. She was charged with harboring farm animals and with cruelty to animals. The sacrifices themselves were saved for a secular future. Said Hill, "All have been adopted out to farms and will be kept as pets."

Terrier: A dog like this saved
the life of his Chihuahua
friend in Barnsley, England.

DOG HERO

Man's best friend may be the dog, but sometimes a dog is better off with another dog. Take the case of Percy the Chihuahua and Mick the terrier.

In Barnsley, England, recently, Percy accompanied his owner, Christine Harrison, on a visit to her parents' home. But the tiny canine refused to stay in the yard; he darted into the street, where he was hit by a car.

"We couldn't detect a heartbeat, and his eyes were fixed and staring. We were all sure he was dead," says Christine. Distraught, she asked her father to bury her pet. Percy was put in a heavy paper sack and entombed in a two-foot-deep grave in the garden.

But Mick, Christine's parents' dog, refused to leave the grave. Finally he dug up Percy and dragged him, still in the burial sack, to the house. "I had already returned home, and it was a shock to have my parents call with the news that my dog had come back from the dead," explains Christine.

Unconscious but with a faint heartbeat, Percy was rushed to a veterinarian, who surmised that the animal had survived because of air trapped in the burial sack. And not only had Mick saved the Chihuahua by digging him up, the vet pointed out, he had also stimulated the little dog's circulation by giving Percy a lick massage.

Percy has recovered, and Mick was recently nominated for an animal lifesaving award by the Royal Society for the Prevention of Cruelty to Animals.

"The strangest thing about all this was that Mick saved Percy at all," Christine points out. "Those two dogs hate each other. They always have, and they still do."

201

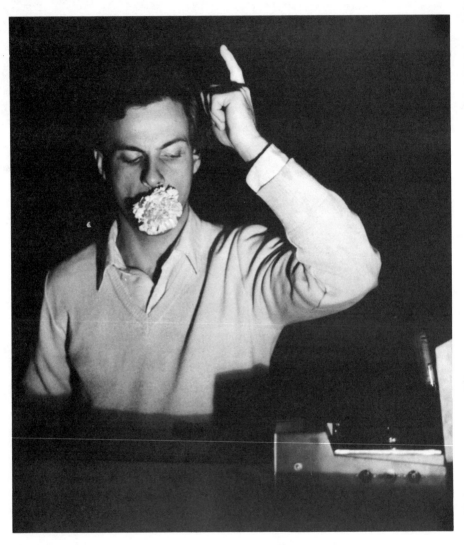

Can flowers and other small objects drop
from the mouth of a psychic?

"No fact is so simple that it is not harder to believe than to doubt at the first presentation."

—*Lucretius*

SCANDAL IN THE SPIRIT WORLD

At thirty-five Paul McElhoney was well on his way to psychic superstardom. Wildly enthusiastic crowds in Britain and Australia flocked to his demonstrations and listened in wonder as the spirit guide Ceros, speaking through McElhoney, uttered words of cosmic wisdom. Selected followers were privileged to sit in a dark room with McElhoney, from whose mouth dropped live goldfish, flowers, and other small objects. And McElhoney also directed United World, a 40,000-member organization dedicated to the dissemination of Ceros's "spirit truths."

Along the way McElhoney accumulated a lot of money—and enough resentment to inspire some fellow Spiritualists to put their suspicions about the young medium to the test. Thus when McElhoney appeared at Spiritualist minister Ronald Baker's home recently, he walked into a trap.

Shortly after his arrival, McElhoney put his tape recorder, which he always used to record his séances, in the darkened séance room. When he went out to mingle with the other guests, though, *News of the World* reporter Alan Whittaker and three Spiritualists entered the room, where they discovered six carnations crammed into the battery compartment of the tape recorder. Later, during the séance, when the flowers miraculously dropped from the medium's mouth, the sitters, unimpressed, switched on the lights and found one carnation still inside the machine.

Angrily refusing to be searched, McElhoney fled into the night and left the telltale tape recorder behind. A picture of it, complete with carnation, was featured in a front-page story of *News of the World.*

In the wake of Britain's biggest psychic scandal in years, McElhoney went into seclusion. A spokesman, claiming the medium was very ill, announced the cancellation of a big United World fest that was to be held in London. There is now talk in Spiritualist circles of a "test séance"—one last chance for McElhoney to prove himself—but so far nothing has come of it.

"Sometimes spirits will write on a blackboard. The board isn't seen, only the white chalk letters. The medium doesn't provide the blackboard. It materializes. But then, the medium doesn't provide transportation for these spirits. He doesn't send a car or plane. Spirits provide their own transportation and their own blackboard."

—*Kenny Kingston*

CODES FROM BEYOND

When the magician Harry Houdini died on Halloween in 1926, it was widely rumored that he had prepared a coded message and that he would communicate the key to that code "from the other side" if it was possible. Even today mediums and psychics hold séances on Halloween and regularly announce that they have received the Houdini message. But reports are so muddled, it is agreed that Houdini's message, if it ever existed, has never been received.

Now Arthur Berger, president of Survival Research Foundation, has started a mass test to see whether the dead *can* send messages after all. All a prospective participant has to do is write to the Survival Research Foundation, P.O. Box 8565, Pembroke Pines, FL 33024. He will then receive a three-page questionnaire and instructions for preparing a coded message of his own.

Here's how it works: Go to the dictionary—preferably a large, unabridged dictionary—and pick a word at random. Consecutively number each letter in the word and in the definition that follows it. Then pick a short phrase or message and substitute numbers for the letters in the phrase.

The key word should then be committed to memory, not written down or told to anyone else. Finally the questionnaire, a photograph of yourself, and the encoded message—along with some personal object or a tape recording of your voice—are sent to the foundation's headquarters. When the foundation has been notified of your death, it sends the photograph or one of the other items to one of a group of psychics.

"We don't identify the subject, and we try to use European psychics with American subjects and vice versa to cut down the possibility of contact between the psychic and subject while the subject is still alive," says Berger. "The psychic tries to receive a key word that will break the code. And if you're out there, you try to send it."

Berger concedes that it would be possible to break the code by normal means, but he considers this highly improbable. "Besides," he says, "we will need more than a couple of successes before we can claim strong evidence for survival."

Any luck yet? "Of course, the subject has to die before the experiment really gets started," Berger explains. "Only one of our hundred or so participants has died so far, and we still haven't gotten the key word from her."

This talented Taurus will not get the job because
his sign says he's lazy and dumb.

ZODIAC
DISCRIMINATION

Your astrological sign
could be keeping you
from getting that job,
according to political
scientist Ralph Bastedo of the State University of New York at Stony Brook.
"In fact," he says, "such discrimination is so common, it's been going on at, of
all places, Ralph Nader's Public Citizen in Washington, D.C."

Though Nader's group claims to be the "watchdog of America," agency
official Joan Claybrook admits that she likes to use the stars as a point of
discussion in job interviews. For example, she explains, "If an applicant is
Pisces, I mention that one of their characteristics is that they often go in two
different directions, which leads to the question of whether they have this
problem."

And Claybrook isn't alone. In a recent study, for instance, Bastedo found
that Berkeley students suffered zodiac discrimination when seeking employment in the San Francisco Bay area. The students say that if they're a Taurus
or Scorpio, employers just won't hire them. Bastedo reports: "Taurus is supposed to be lazy and dumb; Scorpio, evil and manipulative. But when they
choose signs with more favorable traits, like Aquarius, which supposedly indicates a genius on a never-ending quest for truth, they get the jobs."

Bastedo points out that those who use the zodiac to evaluate job seekers
usually go undetected. These employers screen and reject job applicants in
private, he says, and how many people ever suspect they were disqualified
because of a birth date?

It's possible to synchronize your heartbeat with the beat of a metronome.

MUSICAL HEARTTHROBS

While lying on his living room couch and listening to music, a Minneapolis psychologist taught himself to beat his heart to the rhythms of jazz, country, and rock and roll. He claims he can even produce two heartbeats for one musical beat, creating a percussion background.

The virtuoso is Avi Yellin, forty-six, director of research at the University of Minnesota's child and adolescent psychiatry division. Yellin can synchronize his heart with a metronome clicking between 60 and 140 beats per minute, says colleague David Lykken, a psychophysiologist. He has done so in the lab for up to forty minutes and at home for indefinite periods of time.

"If one man can do it, other people as well should be able to influence heart rhythm and blood pressure," adds another colleague, University of Minnesota cardiologist Jay Cohn. Despite preliminary psychological tests, including measurement of brain waves and blood pressure, Cohn does not yet understand the mechanisms by which Yellin voluntarily beats his heart.

Although Cohn doesn't understand this special skill, Yellin himself has a theory: He says he may be linking the brain's cortical areas, which direct higher functions, with subcortical regions, which control internal organs. "There might be a way," he suggests, "to instruct the cortex to communicate with an organ other than the brain, retrieve information, send it back to the cortex, and translate it into a language we can understand."

If this man tries to attack you, just run him over.

MOTORING SCUM

O ur highways are filled with hordes of degenerates and psychopaths," says George Eriksen, a veteran of demolition derbies. "Anybody can be attacked by human scum."

The author of *Getaway,* a manual on driving techniques for escape and evasion, Eriksen points out that a motorist can avoid such scum by drilling a hole in his car's exhaust manifold and welding a can of castor oil to it. The castor oil is installed under the dashboard and connected to a hand pump, Eriksen explains. "So if your car is being followed, you can blind your pursuer with smoke by pumping the oil into your exhaust."

But if you're the kind of motorist who doesn't like punching holes into a new Porsche, Eriksen has some advice for you as well. "Human scum won't normally chase you down the street anyway," he claims. "Instead they'll stand with automatic weapons at roadblocks and get you when you stop." To avoid them, just use the "bootleggers' turn." Here's how: "Simply approach the blockade at thirty miles an hour and crank the steering wheel to half a full turn," says Eriksen. "Then hit the emergency brake until your vehicle skids into a ninety-degree angle. Release the brake, straighten the steering wheel, and hit the gas hard to swing the car to a one-hundred-eighty-degree U-turn."

Since the turn causes incredible wear and tear on your tires, Eriksen warns, "you should practice this maneuver only on a rented car. Just don't tell the rental company what you're planning to do."

AIRPORT FOR EXTRATERRESTRIALS

If extraterrestrials visit Earth sometime soon, where will they land? The White House lawn? The Grand Canyon? Perhaps the Kremlin? Better guess again.

A close encounter of the third kind will occur on the slope of Oriental Mountain, eighty miles south of Mexico City, claims Antonio Vazquez Alva, the man who is building an airport for extraterrestrials there. Alva, forty-four, is a faith healer and president of the occultist Mexican Futurology and Imagination Group.

The airport, which is nearing completion, has a small landing field with a rainbow of signal lights, and there is a modest terminal building where the extraterrestrials and humans can get to know one another. Alva was instructed to build the project, he claims, by an advance party of extraterrestrials from a world "in the fourth dimension."

"They look like humans," Alva says of the alien beings, "but are much more beautiful and shine like angels. Some of them are six feet tall," he adds, "and others are very small—only six inches high."

The extraterrestrials will land at the airport when it is complete, Alva asserts. "These are superior beings with a solution for peace on Earth," he adds, "and they will fulfill us in a way that religion has not."

209

Is there a figure in this rock?

CAVE MOVIES

Italian scriptwriter Piero Tellini was walking near a cave in Ansedonia, Italy, some twenty years ago when he stumbled upon a small, carved stone. That night a storm cast his room into darkness, Tellini recalls, and he began rotating the stone idly in front of his flashlight. Suddenly he says, "an incredible three-dimensional shadow of a primitive beast-man leaped on the wall, its mouth gesticulating and its pupils moving wildly."

That experience changed Tellini's life. He compromised a brilliant movie career, he claims, "to roam the hills looking for stones," while friends "Fellini and Dino De Laurentiis were in their comfortable homes looking for stories."

Immersing himself in archaeology, Tellini soon hypothesized that cavemen had developed the technique of working stone not as a mere pastime but as a sophisticated artistic endeavor. "By manipulating the stones in the right light at a certain speed and angle, the cave dweller could project a succession of images—a short story," the filmmaker explains. "One English stone, for example, shows a hooded figure plunging a knife into a victim; another shows a couple moving into an embrace."

The discovery gave Tellini "a spiritual high. I could've been a monk," he says. But though he believed he had discovered dozens of priceless relics, the few scientists who sat through a viewing saw nothing. Yet Tellini explains, "In the darkest hours, when the whole world was against me, I had only to examine the stones to be happy again."

Finally, Tellini says, there was a breakthrough: He captured the images on video. Nonetheless, he admits, those who saw the tape were still baffled. Metropolitan Museum curator Lois Katz, for one, found it "stimulating but incomprehensible." And *Omni* editor Dick Teresi says, "I couldn't see a thing. He even had trouble working the tape machine. It's hard to believe he was once a filmmaker."

Now, however, Tellini claims that one "Professor Gaietto, a paleontologist from Genoa, has verified that the stones are artifacts dating back to 350,000 B.C." Gaietto does in fact hold that opinion. When asked for his university affiliation, though, he said, "I've studied prehistoric art for twenty-five years, but I'm not a professor. I sell antiques."

Do E.T.'s commune with the deaf and blind?

> "Luddites and anti-
> intellectuals do not master
> the differential equations
> of thermodynamics or the
> biochemical cures of
> illness. They stay in thatched
> huts and die young."
>
> —*E. O. Wilson*

E.T.'S AND THE DEAF

When young William Ortiz fell from a horse in Bucaramanga, Colombia, his chin struck a stone, shattering the bone in his ears and rendering him deaf. Yet Ortiz claims his hearing has slowly returned.

How? "With the help of aliens," explains Center for UFO Studies (CUFOS) investigator Virgilio Sánchez-Ocejo of Miami. This may be the first time, says Sánchez-Ocejo, that extraterrestrials have communicated with a deaf-mute.

Sánchez-Ocejo read about Ortiz in a 1979 CUFOS newsletter and later found him working as a freelance portrait artist in a Las Vegas hotel lobby. Though Ortiz was unable to speak, he did paint a picture documenting his first encounter with aliens. Says Sánchez-Ocejo, "Ortiz told me that these creatures have been following him all his life—even in Las Vegas."

Though Ortiz can't explain exactly how the E.T.'s restored his hearing, he claims he has visited the alien base in Bucaramanga. "But I can't go and verify his claim," Sánchez-Ocejo says, "because I'm a Cuban exile, and if I went to Colombia, the Cuban communists would kill me."

What does J. Allen Hynek, head of the national CUFOS office in Evanston, Illinois, think of all this? "I saw right off the bat that this would be tremendously time-consuming to investigate, and I dropped it," he says. "Not only is Ortiz a deaf-mute, he's unable to express himself even on paper. When he writes down answers to questions, he makes this unintelligible scrawly thing."

Sánchez-Ocejo nonetheless contends that the Ortiz case inspired him to produce the nation's first UFO radio show devoted to "the special relationship between aliens and the handicapped . . . I've discovered many cases where aliens have helped the blind to see and cripples to walk," he says, "which proves that extraterrestrials recognize the disabled as people."

Transplanted alien: Now there's a club just for him.

EXTRATERRESTRIALS ONLY

Is it because you're far from home that you feel miserably earthbound? Tired of that human disguise? Then you need Extraterrestrials Only (E.O.), the first organization for transplanted aliens. Membership includes an official alien I.D. card and a chance to meet other creatures like yourself. That at least is the promise made by E.O. founder Andrew Ferguson, a New Hampshire real estate agent who claims that after only three months in operation, he's registered 283 aliens, mainly from Venus.

Ferguson believes that aliens are like homosexuals were during the earliest stages of the gay liberation movement. "They fear ridicule," he says, "and that's why they need a bona fide human like me to bring them out of the closet."

Eventually, Ferguson says, he hopes to establish a nationwide network of E.O. centers to help aliens cope with the problems of the human world. "For example," he explains, "I got a letter from an eight-year-old boy whose mother was upset because he joined my group. She was afraid he'd take his extraterrestrial origins too far and lose sight of who *she* thought he was." But E.O., he says, could provide group therapy to help the family accept the boy and overcome the difficulty of explaining to relatives, "My son is a Martian."

For information write E.O., P.O. Box 355, Intervale, NH 03845; don't forget to include your alien name and address, planet, and galaxy.

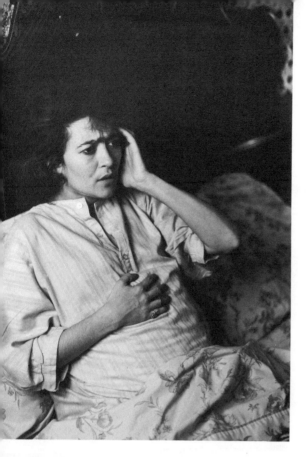

Nightmares may warn pregnant women of the trials and tribulations to come.

DREAM BABIES

Could the dreams of pregnant women hold clues about their unborn babies' health? According to Robert Van de Castle, the answer may be yes. The dreams of pregnancy, says Van de Castle, may predict such things as length of labor and even the likelihood of postpartum depression.

The theory, explains Van de Castle, a psychologist at Blue Ridge Hospital in Charlottesville, Virginia, "is based on the idea that any malfunctioning in the body usually doesn't register during the day. But at night we are like a tuned-in radio. We can better process messages from our body *without* all the disruptive static that comes across in the waking hours."

To document this hypothesis, Van de Castle is currently soliciting dreams from pregnant women, and he's already noted certain patterns. In the early months expectant mothers dream of small animals like fish and kittens. But by the last trimester, there is a seven-fold increase in references to the baby. Some women dream of rejecting or ignoring their new child—and that may prove to be a clue to the development of postpartum depression.

While nightmares about unborn children usually indicate nothing more than common anxiety, says Van de Castle, some women have frightening dreams that appear to be portents of danger. For example, one woman dreamed that her baby was floating on a cloud and waving good-bye. She suffered a miscarriage a few days later. "I've heard a lot of tragic stories from women who dreamed about their babies' deaths or about birth defects, and the dreams came true," he adds. "There seems to be some kind of internal communication."

Despite Van de Castle's evidence, Atlanta obstetrician Julian Fuerst disagrees. "I cannot recall in seventeen years of practice any woman who ever told me of even one dream that was so vivid or bothersome that she worried about it," he says. "And I've never heard of a woman having a dream that in some way predicted the outcome of her pregnancy."

Van de Castle, however, insists that the results of his study may be of practical use to expectant mothers: "If a pregnant woman has dreams that are very vivid and dramatic," he says, "it may be that she needs to have herself checked out by a doctor."

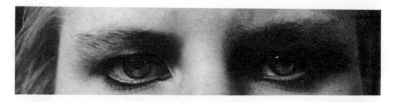

Inspired by the plight of a former beauty queen
who scratched her cornea with an eye pencil,
a Las Vegas doctor has invented permanent eyeliner.

PERMANENT EYELINER

There's new hope for the terminally vain. Using the latest in microsurgical techniques, a Las Vegas ophthalmologist has developed a permanent eyeliner. Known as Permalid, the makeup represents—in the words of its inventor, Dr. Giora P. Angres, of North Las Vegas Hospital—"the start of high-tech cosmetics . . . eventually making it possible for every woman to be beautiful with a minimum of effort."

Inspired by the plight of a former beauty queen whose failing eyesight caused her to scratch her cornea with an eye pencil, Angres worked for seven years to develop his procedure. The operation itself is performed using a special microsurgical tool to implant a pigment in the dermis, the layer of flesh directly beneath the skin. The surgery, which Angres bills as "painless," takes thirty minutes and requires nothing more than local anesthesia. Results can last as long as ten years.

Although there is an undeniable element of wackiness about all this, Angres says that the procedure *does* have serious medical applications. Permalid can aid people with poor vision as well as arthritics who can't raise their hands. Moreover, since Permalid keeps eye pencils away from eyes, it also helps prevent ocular infections.

Currently, says Angres, Permalid comes in two stylish earth tones: gray and brown. But what if a patient turns out to be a punk rocker requesting cadaver purple or metal-flake zebra stripes? Angres pooh-poohs the idea. "If punk rockers ask for this operation," he says, "they'll probably ask for drugs too."

Do crocodiles stalk the sewers of Cairns?

STORM-DRAIN CROCODILES

It's an old story: Tiny alligators owned by New Yorkers grew too large for comfort, so they were flushed down the toilet. Instead of succumbing, though, the reptiles flourished in the city's sewers, where they live and breed to this very day. The story is only a rumor, of course, but a similar account of crocodiles in Cairns, Australia, may have more validity.

According to Cairns police sergeant Jim Buttsworth, most of the animals are fairly small—three to four feet long—and rarely cause residents any problems. But at least one croc seems to have developed a taste for people. Twenty-one-year-old Leon Philips was walking along a main city street recently when a crocodile locked its jaws around his leg. According to police sources, Philips kicked the reptile away, thanks to his heavy cowboy boots and with the help of a nearby cabdriver.

"The croc dived back into the drain and is still at large," Sergeant John MacDonald later explained. "We've issued an all-points bulletin for it."

But how did the fresh-water crocodiles end up as urban inhabitants in the first place? Sergeant Buttsworth has a familiar explanation: "We think somebody had a small croc or two, and when the crocs got too large, they released the animals into the storm drains."

The poor now sell body parts in order to make a buck.

SPARE-PARTS SALE

Jeff Nicoll, a twenty-seven-year-old self-described jack-of-all-trades placed this simple ad in the Tampa *Tribune:* KIDNEY FOR SALE. $30,000. CALL AFTER 5 P.M. Out of work and desperate for money, Nicoll was trying to cash in on the highly publicized shortage of organs by selling one of his own.

While he didn't find any takers, Nicoll isn't alone. According to Amy Peele, president of the Chicago-based North American Transplant Coordinators Organization, "The whole thing is growing to fad proportions. I get five calls on the subject a week."

A proposed United States law, notes Peele, would make the sale of body organs illegal. But already people like Harold Hedrick, a forty-seven-year-old carpet-factory worker in rural Dalton, Georgia, have retained lawyers to help them sell organs and research their rights. "There are plenty of people who need a kidney and would be glad to pay the twenty-five thousand dollars plus expenses that I'm asking," says Hendrick, who wants the money to buy a fast-food restaurant. "I'm real healthy, and this is a way for me to help someone while they help me. It makes me feel sad to hear that someone has died waiting for a kidney while I have one just ready to go. The problem," he adds, "is finding a doctor to do the operation."

But doctors and other critics of organ selling list a host of possible horrors: Droves of destitute people might undergo potentially dangerous surgery for the promise of quick cash. And since many patients are in low-income brackets, they could become the victims of a bidding war in which only the wealthiest could afford organs. Finally, donors could develop diseases in their remaining organs, making them candidates for transplants.

These fears, though, have not stopped people from trying to sell parts of their bodies. "After that first ad appeared, we were deluged with people offering other organs," says Yvonne Shinholster, of the Tampa *Tribune.* "It's hard to believe, but there are people who want to sell lungs, eyes—even arms and legs."

"As I studied the magnified
surface of the moon upon
the screen . . . a small
animal ran across the area I
was observing. I could
see that it was four-legged
and furry, but its speed
prevented me from
identifying it."

—*George Adamski*

Doctors, teachers, and truckdrivers bend spoons in Malibu.

SPOON BENDING PARTIES

When Jack Houck, engineer of McDonnell Douglas, throws a party, no one plays Pin the Tail on the Donkey. Instead each guest is given a spoon and told to yell "Bend, bend, bend!"

"In minutes," says Houck, "guests physically generate heat in the metal, spoons flop over, and eyeballs bulge like popcorn."

According to Houck's friend, Oregon engineer Walter Uphoff, those attending the parties are skeptical at first, "like my six-year-old granddaughter," says Uphoff. "But once she saw how easy it was, she bent five spoons in a night." In fact, says Uphoff, Japanese television had picked up on the spoon-bending craze, broadcasting a weekly party show and encouraging millions of Japanese to destroy dinnerware in the privacy of their homes.

Houck points out that soft silver spoons bend the fastest—in two minutes as opposed to fifteen for stainless steel. "In one night," he says, "I mangled an entire inheritance of silverware from my grandparents. I bet they never imagined they'd be making a donation to science."

But the future of spoon bending, Houck adds, lies in space. He hopes to invite the space-shuttle astronauts to his next party. After all, he points out, "If the astronauts were stuck in space without a wrench, they could throw a little party and bend metal to make a needed, lifesaving repair."

Over the last two years Houck has thrown more than a hundred spoon-bending parties for two thousand people. Guests, including doctors, teachers, and truck drivers, learn about the parties through word of mouth or local newspaper ads. "It's free," he says, "and they've all gone on to throw parties of their own."

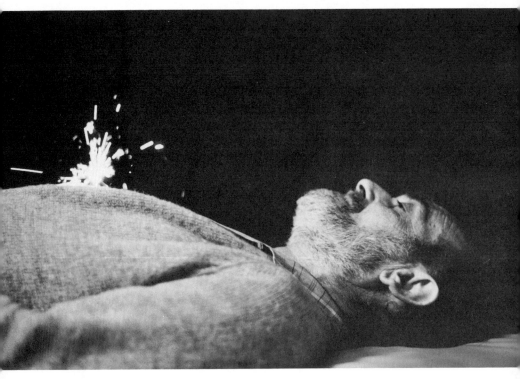

The nitro patches worn by heart patients
may turn into firecrackers.

EXPLODING HEART

Nitroglycerin is a deadly explosive. But its derivatives are also used in the treatment of heart disease. Film patches soaked in inert nitro compounds, in fact, can be attached to the skin, sending the drug through the body to expand blood vessels and fend off attacks. The patches, introduced to the market in 1982, have just one drawback: They can turn into firecrackers.

The problem emerged last year at the Naval Regional Medical Center in Charleston, South Carolina, where physician John Babka was trying to save a heart-attack victim who was wearing a nitro patch. Using standard medical procedure, Babka applied electrical shocks to the patient's chest. But as the electricity flowed, Babka heard a loud bang. "There was a flash and a puff of yellow smoke," he says, "and the patch turned black."

Although the explosion didn't harm his patient (the man died subsequently of a heart attack), Babka set out to determine its cause. First he fastened a nitro patch to a corpse. Then he applied electric shocks to the chest. He found that the patch went pop only when it received a direct jolt of electricity. Then, cutting open the burnt patch, Babka found a layer of aluminum foil. Obviously, he concluded, "when the paddle delivering the shock met the aluminum, it behaved like a screwdriver in a live socket."

Babka forwarded his results to the company manufacturing the patches, CIBA-GEIGY Pharmaceuticals in Summit, New Jersey. Responding to Babka's alert, the company's communications manager, David Catlett, says, "We're now putting labels on the patches, warning doctors to remove them before applying a shock. But since this occurrence is rare, we're not recalling the product. We don't know how many patches are out there anyhow."

Babka, however, would like to see doctors warned as soon as possible. He's had only two reports of exploding patches this year, but, he points out, "When a person's heart stops beating, every second of treatment is vital. So if a doctor is momentarily distracted from his patient because of an unexpected explosion, it could mean that person's death."

Undetected alien: He surrounds himself with exotic, high-tech gadgetry.

ALIENS AMONG US

Do you know someone who constantly misuses everyday items? Is his skin ice cold or too hot? Does his mood change when you turn on the microwave oven? Does he own plenty of exotic high-tech gadgetry? And is he forever poring over newspapers, magazines, scientific journals, and mail-order catalogs?

Beware. These could be telltale signs of a cleverly disguised extraterrestrial, says Brad Steiger, coauthor with his wife Francie of *The Star People,* a nonfiction book about Earthlings descended from aliens.

Brad Steiger believes that humankind may actually be a sort of "biology lab project" for some distant alien race that sends observers to learn our ways and gather information about us. "They want to see whether we are developing a scientific, technological, and spiritual evolution," he suggests.

What to do if you spot some oddball absentmindedly eating french fries with a spoon or methodically speed-reading his way through a stack of magazines? "Since the alien would be here just as an observer," Brad Steiger says, "take no action. I would hate for the Ku Klux Klan or some group like that to start hunting aliens."

THE
BATS

First it was *The Birds,* then *Killer Bees,* and now it's time to watch out for the bats. On a recent Friday the thirteenth (of course) a student at a junior high school in Lake City, Florida, found a dead Mexican freetail bat on the floor of the school gymnasium. Analysis showed that the bat was rabid, which quickly brought local health officials. They quarantined the gym, then crept in one dark night and flipped the lights on. "We had to start ducking," says Columbia county environmental health director Steve Knight. "Those bats were *everywhere.*"

Knight found that the bats—some five hundred of them—had squeezed through tiny spaces between electrical junctions and had roosted inside the gym's double-block concrete walls. "As far as they were concerned," Knight says, "it was just like a cave." Outside a row of mercury-vapor lamps attracted insects on which the bats fed. "They had everything they needed," Knight concluded. "They had their housing, and they had their dinner all laid out for them. It was bat paradise."

The school board quickly called in a local pest-control company, which began wiping out the invaders, who were by then perching on the steel girders and chattering away behind the gym's electronic scoreboard. First the pest-control people tried putting mothballs in every hole they could find, but the bats simply pushed the mothballs aside when they wanted to get out. Next they tried shooting the critters with .22-caliber rifles, but the cost of individual executions was ten dollars per bat. "They could have gone on doing that forever," says Knight, "and it still wouldn't have solved the problem."

In the meantime the invasion had caused quite a stir. Alarmed by statistics that showed that as many as 40 percent of the bats could be rabid, the townspeople peppered Knight and the school board with angry phone calls. "A couple of times," Knight admits, "I felt like I was in a Frankenstein movie, where all the villagers have got the torches lighted because they're going to burn down the mansion and get rid of the monsters."

In the wake of this public outcry, the pest-control company finally decided to get mean. They sealed up every possible exit, then pulled their trucks up to the gym and pumped carbon monoxide from the exhausts into the gym walls, turning the erstwhile bat cave into a gas chamber. According to Knight, "that whole place is now a bat cemetery. It's like the pyramids of Egypt: one big tomb."

British ghost: He doesn't realize he's an apparition.

GHOST WALK

Margaret Royal was out on a stroll one afternoon when she passed an acquaintance and nodded hello. Nothing strange about that. But when she got home and opened the newspaper, she discovered that her friend had been dead for a week! Muses Royal, "I must've seen her ghost."

But that's no big deal for the woman who has earned the title "the Ghost Lady of Bath." The author of three compendiums of British ghosts, Royal claims that her hometown of Bath is so awash with spirits that she has organized "a ghost walk" around town. As tourists follow the "ghost circuit" from one haunt to another, she says, they feel sudden shivers, smell hovering rotten odors, and even see apparitions.

Take the sword-bearing macho ghost, for instance. "He's revealed himself to only a few fortunate men," Royal says, "but many visitors complain of a sudden chill near his house, indicating he was killed in a duel nearby." Another ghost thumps people on the back, and yet another—a tall woman in black—appears by a bed and rips off all the blankets.

Where do the ghosts come from? "When you see or sense a ghost," Royal explains, "you go through a bend or chink leading to another time. Some ghosts may even hail from the future," she notes, "and *those* entities may think that *we're* the spirits."

226

SEARCH FOR JASON

Greek mythology tells of the heroic Jason and his crew of Argonauts. This courageous team, legend has it, fought the Amazons, half-bird/half-woman creatures called Harpies, and other fantastic monsters on their perilous voyage to retrieve the Golden Fleece. But could there be any truth to this ancient and amazing tale?

Absolutely, according to adventurer and Oxford scholar Tim Severin, who has authored eight books on exploration. Severin and his crew of twenty in fact have vowed to retrace the ancient route and locate the kingdom of Colchis, home of Jason's sorceress-wife Medea.

Severin's group set sail this past March in a ship named after its legendary counterpart, the *Argo.* A recreation of the ancient Greek escort vessel, the boat is fifty-four feet and nine inches long, nine feet and four inches wide. It is made of pine, coated with pitch, and topped with a single flax sail.

The team is traveling from the Greek city of Volos, thought to be the site of Jason's hometown of Pegasae, to the Black Sea, which Severin contends is the "Unfriendly Sea" of mythical fame. From there they will head up to the Soviet Republic of Georgia, where, Severin speculates, the kingdom of Colchis might have flourished. His reasoning: Medea was noted for her magic potions, and drugs have historically passed by Georgia on their way to Europe.

Carter Phillips, chairman of the classical studies department at Vanderbilt University, points out that if Jason really existed, he lived about three thousand years ago, during the Bronze Age. "We have no written history of that era," he says. "But there is always a possibility that there is a historical kernel of truth to these myths. In fact the trade routes of the time may well explain Jason's voyage. There's no reason to think that Severin's ideas are way off base. And it will be very interesting to see what he comes up with."

Archetypal nightmare: This man is only dreaming, but in the
morning he'll claim he was abducted by aliens.

"UFO witnesses
weave their abduction stories
from haunting but
submerged memories of birth."

UFO
UPDATE

Editor's note: California ufologist Alvin Lawson writes about his investigation of the abduction phenomenon, below:

A group of volunteers were hypnotized in a hushed California hospital and then were asked to imagine detailed encounters with extraterrestrials: One woman fantasized a creature that probed her with a beam from its single eye. A nurse saw herself levitated from her car into a spaceship operated by fetuslike beings with bumpy skin. And a student imagined being whisked into a cavernous UFO through a tunnel of brilliant light.

The researchers—hypnotist William McCall, ufologist John de Herrera, and I—had chosen these subjects because they knew little or nothing about classic UFO lore; we expected their stories to differ drastically from those told by allegedly real UFO abductees like the legendary Betty and Barney Hill. But to our surprise the fabricated encounters were virtually identical to the "real" ones.

To us these findings mean one thing: UFO abduction stories stem not from meetings with aliens but from an inner fantasy world that may be common to us all. The root of such fantasy is the trauma of birth itself.

Indeed most UFO abduction stories are loaded with birth images: tunnels, womb-shaped rooms, cervixlike doorways. Just as the fetus moves through the tortuous birth tunnel into a big, bright room, where adults handle it, so the abductee levitates through an ominous tunnel of light into a UFO's vast interior, where strange creatures probe its body.

But most UFO researchers have ignored the implications of our work. For instance, in a recent book author Budd Hopkins says he and a colleague studied dozens of people who reported periods of temporary amnesia. Under hypnosis, thirty-six of them "remembered" elaborate abductions involving fetuslike aliens, medical examinations, and piercing light. Hopkins contends that his subjects were kidnapped by aliens, but as far as my research team is concerned, *Missing Time* actually supports the birth-trauma theory.

And we believe we can prove it. First, abduction stories told under hypnosis can be scrutinized for echoes of an individual's birth history. When a subject says an alien's metal clamp held and twisted him, for example, we can try to discover whether or not he had a forceps-aided delivery. If so, he's remembering his birth. If the subject reports an easy passage into a chamber of light instead of a tight, twisting canal, we can try to learn whether he was caesarean-born. If so, then the birth-trauma hypothesis would hold true once again.

Finally a bit of recent research even suggests that birth might account for the period of "missing time." Scientists have found that oxytocin, the hormone that floods the mother and fetus during birth, causes amnesia in laboratory animals. Doctors say the substance probably causes amnesia in people too.

One-dollar bills have been frightening county officers around the country.

MYSTERY MONEY

Mysterious envelopes containing crisp one-dollar bills have baffled Florida officials from the Gulf Panhandle down to the Keys. At last count, fifty-three municipal managers have received the envelopes, which bear no return address or message, save for a Baltimore, Maryland, postmark.

Opa-Locka City Manager Albert Chandler, for instance, reported that his office received two "offerings" mailed a year apart, the last in early 1984. Each dollar was pressed between two pieces of green cardboard.

"We never determined who the benevolent individual was," says Chandler, who put the money in the city safe. "My initial thought was that whoever sent the money had heard about our town's financial problems."

"When I first got my dollar, I just assumed someone wanted to repay a police officer for loaning them a gallon of gas, or something like that," adds Tobie Wilson, Mayor of Medley. "Then I found out all these other people were receiving bills too. Who knows? Maybe someone's trying to put a hex on us."

Hex or not, no one has a clue as to who sent the money. But when word spread about the Florida mailings, community officials in other parts of the country announced that they too had received the donations. A couple of crisp dollar bills reached Maryland city managers and mayors; several California towns were put on the mailing list as well.

While the mystery may never be solved, recipients of the unsolicited currency are taking their windfall in stride. Comments Greenacres, Florida, City Administrator Wally Douthwaite, "I've already spent the dollar."

"I've confirmed a lot of
poltergeist activity while
couples are engaged in
violent sex."

—*Peter Underwood*

Kinky alien: Did she seduce a youth in the fields of Brazil?

EXTRATERRESTRIAL SEX

UFO abduction stories are usually standard: Visiting aliens kidnap their terrified human victims and subject them to a medical exam. Then they give a few words of kindly advice and send them on their way.

But now, out of the Center for Flying Saucer Research in Brazil, comes an abduction story with a twist. Not only was the victim kidnapped and examined by aliens, he was seduced as well, the center reports.

The encounter, covered in a recent issue of the *MUFON* (Mutual UFO Network) *Journal,* allegedly occurred on April 13, 1979, near the city of Maringa in southern Brazil. It all began when Jocelino De Mattos, twenty-one, and his brother, Roberto Carlos, thirteen, glimpsed a strange star in the sky above the city streets. Soon drawn to a nearby field, the brothers fell to the ground before a hovering UFO. Then they lost consciousness. When they woke up hours later, the UFO was gone.

The report eventually came to the attention of Brazilian ufologist A. J. Gevaerd, who convinced Jocelino to undergo hypnosis in an attempt to recall the experience. On the hypnotist's couch, Jocelino soon remembered boarding the UFO. "The aliens asked me to lie down, and as I did so, they examined me," he said. "Then, after the examination, they collected sperm [through a tube]. Then they made me sit down on a kind of table. They put some instruments in my head, and they spoke among themselves in a language that I did not understand."

Jocelino stalled before continuing his testimony, Gevaerd reports. But finally, with encouragement from the hypnotist, he continued. "After some minutes a woman arrived in the room. She touched me. She caressed me, and it excited me. Then we started to make love."

The woman looked human, the young abductee added, and he was able to complete the act. The aliens released him sometime later, after explaining (telepathically, of course) that they had come on a mission of peace.

What's to be made of all this? Bob Pratt, editor of the *MUFON Journal,* looked into the case during a field trip to Brazil. He discovered that in Brazil UFO abductees *do* report sexual seductions every so often. He also met members of the De Mattos family and was able to speak to the younger boy. "Evidently something did happen, since other family members reported sightings that night," Pratt states. "I have no reason to doubt the claims, and I don't think the case was a hoax."

When a pet predeceases its master, it reappears in the form of a ghost.

PET AFTERLIFE

Bonds between people and their pets are often strong. Dogs have tracked misplaced masters across miles of unknown landscape; wealthy spinsters have lavished fortunes upon beloved animal companions; and people have even been buried alongside their cats. Now Ontario sociologist Ian Currie, author of *You Cannot Die,* says that not even death can destroy such devotion.

"If there is a strong attachment between pet and master, the two are likely to be united in death," according to Currie, who says he's documented such cases "in séances with reputable mediums." The deceased, he adds, have rendezvoused with dogs, cats, and, in one instance, a horse, and one woman frolicked with her dog, also deceased, only minutes after she died.

When a pet predeceases its master, Currie notes, it reappears in the form of a ghost and haunts the master's house. "Sometimes the pet sticks around because it's attached to the master," he says, "and sometimes it is simply unaware of the fact that it has died."

234

TURKEY CHORUS

Musician Jim Nollman is so impressed with what animals have to say that he has dedicated his life to composing songs for them.

Nollman's career began in an Indian village in New Mexico, where he had gone to seek solitude after years of playing the guitar at shows and clubs. Next door lived a family who owned a turkey. "I was practicing the flute when I noticed that if I hit certain notes the turkey would gobble," Nollman says. Soon he learned to "ride the turkey's energy," teaching it to join in a flute/turkey duet. Elated, he took the discovery home to San Francisco, where a farmer allowed him to organize three hundred turkeys into a chorus. The result, called "Music to Eat Thanksgiving Dinner By," became a modest hit on local radio.

Since then Nollman's reputation has spread like seeds around a barnyard. Camping at a California wolf preserve, he learned to sing wolf harmony at the rise of the moon. Later he developed underwater instruments and made music with killer whales and dolphins in Canada, Hawaii, Mexico, and Japan. ("They would come around," he says, "and start jumping whenever I played.") He played the mandolin for buffalo—which silently surrounded him—for ABC television, and he set up a grunting chorus of howler monkeys for educational TV. In 1982 he produced an album that featured the squeaks, gobbles, and barks of Jim Nollman making music with whales, turkeys, and wolves.

Now he's preparing for a project to cap them all: filling a boat with his electronic equipment to seek out the most musical animals in the world. He compares the plan to what Jacques Cousteau has done with his ship, the *Calypso*. "This boat can be a new-age *Calypso*," he says. "What Cousteau did for ecology, we plan to do for interspecies communication."

HAUNTED
PUBS

Teacher's Scotch recently sponsored an investigation of twelve allegedly haunted pubs throughout the United Kingdom. A prize of £1,000 was offered to the pub owner whose establishment was deemed by investigators to be a site of true paranormal activity.

The ghost hunters came up empty-handed, however, and Teacher's donated the money to charity. But that doesn't necessarily mean that ghosts and poltergeists don't reside in some British pubs, according to at least one of the investigators.

"There were many instances where we found very interesting reports of hauntings," notes Debra Dellanoy of Edinburgh University. "But a proper investigation is time-consuming—it involves tracking down stories and trying to come up with a normal cause for the events. And those of us who participated in the Teacher's ghost hunt were at each pub for only a day and a night."

Dellanoy says that in one pub witnesses she rates highly credible reported objects flying around the room. "One man was struck in the head by a flying ashtray. And there were also reports of the paranormal lighting of candles," says Dellanoy. But despite the reported events, nothing happened while the investigators were on hand.

"We sat in pubs and waited for ghosts. We looked for apparitions in cellars. We sat on beds and waited for Victorian children to come through the walls," comments Teacher's publicity director David Dorman. "Apparently ghosts just don't turn up on demand."

ROBOT
EVOLUTION

Taking up where Charles Darwin left off, a scientist at Carnegie-Mellon's Robotics Institute has linked the future of human evolution to robots and the computer. Within thirty years, according to Hans Moravec, computers will be more intelligent than humans, and robot limbs will be more durable than human ones. The result: People will trade their feeble mortal frames for powerful robot shells and their plodding brains for superintelligent computers.

At first, Moravec says, people will transfer exact replicas of their brain patterns to computer programs. Processed by speedy computers, the programs will enable people to think thousands of times faster than before.

The next evolutionary leap, Moravec says, will occur when superhuman robots give up their desire for individuality and being to share programs. If, for example, a writer wanted to build a cabinet, he or she could save time by borrowing the memory of a carpenter. And hundreds of scientists with access to minds as brilliant as Einstein's would spend their days fathoming the universe.

As people select and discard memories freely, Moravec says, the concept of self will be blurred. Moravec envisions the ultimate merger of all human brains with the brains of other forms of life, both earthly and extraterrestrial. After years of exchange, he says, we might wind up with a single conscious entity whose memory is stored in a vast bank spanning the universe.

"At first I thought
these people had it together,
but then I realized
they really believed this junk."

UFO
UPDATE

She fell into a deep sleep and woke seconds later in a glowing "organic" chamber on the planet Ancore. Her host, a ten-foot-tall creature named Aranon, took her to a small, egg-shaped space-craft, and in just seconds they arrived at Colony Five, a planet for displaced Earthlings. Their next stop was a rocky world with oaklike palm trees and menacing cavemen. Fortunately Aranon uttered a secret word, stopping the savages in their tracks. Then the travelers reentered their spacecraft, arriving at Ancore in a matter of seconds.

That at least was the story told by Christy Dennis, thirty-seven, a house-wife from Phoenix. While meditating at home after breaking her hip in a traffic accident, she says, she momentarily lost consciousness, waking up in another world. Though she blacked out for only a minute on Earth, she claimed she spent fourteen days in space. By the time she returned, her hip had healed so well that she could walk across the room. Afterward she wrote a book about her experiences, sketched the aliens, and drew schematics of the spacecraft and its power drive.

The Dennis story caught the attention of Leo Sprinkle, a counselor at the University of Wyoming and a leading finder of supposedly repressed UFO abduction experiences. Sprinkle accepted Dennis's story and recruited her help in a 1981 conference for abductees.

Participating in the conference, Dennis soon met Dan and Eileen Edwards of UFO Contact Center International, a support group for UFO contactees. "It seemed like a good avenue for me to investigate," says Dennis, who decided to visit the center. "At first I thought these people really had it together. But slowly I began to realize that this was screwy. They really believed this junk, despite a great deal of missing or twisted information."

After Dennis got back from her second week-long session with the Ed-wardses, in fact, she rocked the nation's UFO establishment by admitting that her dramatic "UFO abduction" was a hoax. "I am not a contactee," she told the UFO world in an open letter. "I never had an extraterrestrial experience.

The stories I have told and the book I have written are nothing more than fair science fiction." She concluded her letter with a warning to UFO investigators: "Take a good look at what you are willing to believe. If I could get your attention, how many other frauds have been able to do the same?"

Now, however, Dennis is repudiating her earlier repudiation. She admits she was never abducted by aliens but insists her story was not a hoax. "I was just barking up the wrong tree," she says. "I was meditating, and I simply experienced a space-time continuum shift. When we encounter something alien to our symbolic reference patterns, we have to make up the words to explain it."

Though Dennis can't validate her story, she claims the experience had some tangible results. "My I.Q. went from 110 to 165," she explains, "and I developed a sensitivity to earthquakes, as well as a deep knowledge of nuclear physics."

FRENCH
FLYING SAUCER

Jean-Claude Ladrat, foreman at a small timber firm in southwestern France, has spent the past ten years building a flying saucer in his backyard.

It all began one evening in 1969 as Ladrat, then a merchant seaman on a Scandinavian oil tanker, sailed through the infamous Bermuda Triangle. Ladrat, who had been staring at the stars, was struck with the vision of a magnificent flying saucer. Every detail of the craft's design was revealed, Ladrat says, and the course of his life was clear; he would have to get to work.

Nine months later Ladrat moved to the farmhouse that would become the base for his activities. It took him seven years to build the craft's motor. Situated under the pilot's seat, this cone-shaped engine is made up of eleven panels, each containing forty-nine electromagnetic circuits. It works, says Ladrat, by magnifying the pilot's willpower, thereby generating a force field powerful enough to counteract Earth's gravitational pull.

By 1978, with the motor complete, it was time to start work on the hull—several layers of plywood, plastic sheeting, lead, and aluminum to protect the craft from magnetic and gravitational forces.

Today the *Ladratan One* is almost complete, and the date for its maiden flight is drawing near. Whether or not one shares Ladrat's "minor" doubts about the final success of the venture, one thing is sure: For once photographs of a flying saucer are clear, distinct, and in focus.

GHOST
HUNT

Have you ever seen a ghost or apparition? If so, the American Society for Psychical Research (ASPR), located in New York City, would like to hear a report of the incident.

Most people who see ghosts don't tell anyone for fear of ridicule, according to Dr. Karl Osis, head of ASPR's apparition project. Yet the haunted are beginning to come forward. In a recent Gallup Poll conducted in Great Britain, 14 percent of the people questioned asserted that they had seen apparitions. And in a national opinion poll of Americans, 27 percent of the respondents said they had communicated with the dead.

According to Osis, the society is most interested in hearing about ghosts or apparitions that have been seen by at least two persons, or by one person and a pet. Privacy and confidentiality, Osis adds, are promised to all those who participate in the ASPR project.

HAITIAN ZOMBIES

Late night television is the only place you're likely to see a zombie, one of those mythical human creatures said to have risen from the dead. But now it appears there may be some truth in the legend.

"I am absolutely convinced that zombies exist," says Lamarque Douyton, a physician who has spent the past twenty years attempting to debunk voodoo and related phenomena. "I have seen them for myself." Douyton, chief of psychiatry for the government of Haiti, has examined three zombies, two of whom are still under study at his Port-au-Prince clinic.

"What we have here are cases of flesh-and-blood individuals who have succumbed to a state of apparent death brought on by drugs," Douyton explains. "The people are pronounced dead and are publicly buried, then exhumed and reanimated by the voodoo sorcerers who administered the drugs in the first place." The sorcerers, according to Douyton, are able to enslave most of these zombies for the remainder of their lives by adding minute quantities of the poison to their daily food. On occasion, however, some of them manage to escape.

Although the exact nature of the poison is unknown, Douyton suspects it may be derived from flowers of the genus *Datura*. He has already injected a liquid concoction made from the flower into mice and dogs and has documented a remarkable motor slowdown in their vital signs. This is followed by a comatose state, which lasts anywhere from three to six hours, depending on the dosage administered, after which the experimental animals recover fully.

"We still don't have all the answers," Douyton laments, "but we're trying to unravel this mystery." Mystery or not, the bizarre phenomenon appears to be quite common in Haiti. Indeed the country's penal code states that turning someone into a zombie is tantamount to murder.

BIGFOOT
PRESERVE

Most environmental agencies protect endangered species in reserves where the animals can roam and reproduce, unmolested by man. But in China this compassionate policy has now been extended to the wildest of all wildlife: Bigfoot himself. According to the Chinese journal *Science and Man,* part of the Shennongjia Mountains, in central Hubei Province, have been set aside as preserves for the *ye ren,* those hairy ten-foot-tall redheads the Chinese have allegedly been observing for centuries.

The inspiration behind the new preserve is Li Jian, secretary general of the Wild Man Research Institute in the Hubei city of Wuhan. Although no *ye ren* photographs or other forms of hard evidence have surfaced, Li Jian says, the creature's existence seems more certain with each passing year.

In 1980, for instance, Hubei commune member Pu Xiaoqiu reportedly caught a "little wild man" in an animal trap. "Unfortunately," wrote Li, "the superstitious Pu thought the beast was the reincarnation of a friend who had died two months before, and so set him free." Still, Li claims that as many as 200 nineteen-inch-long footprints have been found on Hubei's Jiongdao Mountain and that Wuhan Medical College has recently examined "hairs of eight kinds of red-haired wild men."

The new preserve in the Shennongjia Mountains is just the beginning, according to Li. The Wild Man Research Institute has plans to extend the search for *ye ren* over the entire country.

> "He raked me with
> beams of hatred as strong as
> the flash of the
> craft supposedly seen by Travis."

UFO
UPDATE

Editor's note: Jeff Wells, a former reporter for the *National Enquirer*, tells how he covered one of the most famous UFO stories in history, below.

Take one haunted young man, a ruthless cowboy, an eccentric professor, and a hard-drinking psychiatrist. Throw them together with a bunch of sensation-seeking reporters in the desert heat. Add a spaceship manned by little men with fishbowl heads, and you have the makings of a B movie.

But in November 1975 this situation was real, and it turned into that celebrated piece of UFO lore known as the Travis Walton case. I was part of this lunacy, and it left me with the whimsical realization that when it comes to big-bucks ufology, proof is the last thing anyone cares about.

According to six witnesses, Travis, a twenty-two-year-old forestry worker, had disappeared in the Arizona woods, running toward the blinding light of a flying saucer. I was one of a team of reporters from the *National Enquirer* sent to intercept Travis after he reappeared five days later, claiming to have been abducted by aliens. Our task: to win the confidence of Travis's cowboy older brother.

The cowboy was one of the meanest, toughest-looking men I've ever seen —a rodeo pro, a light-heavyweight fighter, T-shirt packed with muscle, eyes full of nails, tense, unpredictable. The first time I met him, he leaned against a pickup truck and raked me with beams of cunning and hatred as strong as the flash from the spacecraft that supposedly had terrified his younger brother.

But it turned out that the cowboy could be bought. When he found out the *Enquirer* would offer thousands of dollars to anyone who could prove that aliens had visited our planet, he agreed to hide out with Travis in our motel room.

A professor we got to come from Berkeley, California, would put Travis under hypnosis. Travis was mute, pale, twitching like a cornered animal. But the professor was cooing: "You are not alone. There are many people, more than you could even imagine, who have been chosen to meet them."

Them? We began to worry about the professor.

With history and an offer of $10,000 at stake, Travis spun a ripping yarn of extraterrestrials with skin that looked like mushrooms. But the euphoria vanished when we brought in the state's top polygraph operator, who, after questioning young Travis, said it was the plainest case of lying he had ever heard. I'll never forget the bug-eyed cowboy's screams of rage. "I'll kill the son of a bitch!"

Then a psychiatrist flew in from Colorado. He locked himself in a room with Travis, the cowboy, and a bottle of cognac. When the three staggered out hours later, the psychiatrist had the story: Travis had been acting out a childhood fantasy, nurtured since his father, a UFO cultist, had left him.

As they departed, the cowboy promised that his sick brother would get the care and rest he needed. But as I neared the airport, my radio was broadcasting their amazing tale of an encounter with aliens.

I asked my editors at the *Enquirer* to kill the story of Travis and his coneheads as a warped prank. But a few weeks later it appeared on the front page. And another space hero was born.

"It is a condition which
confronts us—not a theory."

—*Grover Cleveland*

ESP
BELIEVERS

Parapsychologists—the folks who test clairvoyance and telepathy in the laboratory—believe in ESP. That's the not-very-surprising conclusion of two recent surveys of parapsychologists across the country.

According to the first study, conducted by the Parapsychological Association, 88 percent of those who belong to the association believe that ESP has been either "positively" or "probably" demonstrated. The younger members of the organization are less certain, however, with a mere 74 percent professing overwhelming faith. In the second survey, conducted by two professors at the University of Pittsburgh, 68 percent of the parapsychologists questioned said they had "complete" faith in ESP, and 22 percent said their belief in ESP was "strong."

Which professional group is most skeptical when it comes to ESP? Ordinary psychologists. Indeed, according to yet another survey, only 5.5 percent of all psychologists believe in ESP.